Better partnership working

MANAGING AND LEADING IN INTER-AGENCY SETTINGS

Better partnership working

Series editors: Jon Glasby and Helen Dickinson

About the authors

Edward Peck is Professor of Public Services Development and Director of the School of Public Policy at the University of Birmingham. As a former NHS manager of mental health services, an acknowledged expert on the theory and practice of public sector partnerships and a leading practitioner of leadership development in public services, he is probably uniquely placed to write a text on leadership in partnership settings.

Helen Dickinson is a researcher at the Health Services Management Centre, University of Birmingham, with an interest in evaluating the outcomes of health and social care partnerships. Recent research and consultancy work include producing research-based but accessible discussion papers for funders such as the Wanless Review of the funding of adult social care, the NHS Institute and the Care Services Improvement Partnership.

MANAGING AND LEADING IN INTER-AGENCY SETTINGS

Edward Peck and Helen Dickinson

in association with

COMMUNITYcare

First published in Great Britain in 2008 by

The Policy Press
University of Bristol
Fourth Floor, Beacon House
Queen's Road
Bristol BS8 1QU

Tel +44 (0)117 331 4054
Fax +44 (0)117 331 4093
e-mail tpp-info@bristol.ac.uk
www.policypress.org.uk

British Library Cataloguing in Publication Data
A catalogue record for this book is available from the British Library

Library of Congress Cataloging-in-Publication Data
A catalog record for this book has been requested

ISBN 978 1 84742 025 1 paperback

Cover design by In-text Design, Bristol
Printed and bound in Great Britain by MPG Books, Bodmin

Contents

List of tables, figures and boxes   vi
Acknowledgements   viii
List of abbreviations   ix
Preface   xi

1   What are management and leadership and why do   1
they matter in partnerships?

2   What does research tell us?   31

3   Hot topics and emerging issues   59

4   Useful frameworks and concepts   79

5   Recommendations for policy and practice   105

References   107
Index   127

List of tables, figures and boxes

Tables

1.1	A classification of types of networks	18
1.2	Summary of major approaches to leadership	24
2.1	'Classical' and network management compared	36
3.1	Perspectives on organisational governance	63
3.2	Four-stage approach of performance	70
4.1	Differences in characterisation of the NHS and social services partners	85
4.2	The 'democratic deficit' in partnerships	90
4.3	The findings and implications of research by Fitzgerald et al on adoption of evidence-based practice	102

Figures

1.1	Depth versus breadth of relationship	9
1.2	Conceptualising networks around four basic ways of organising	19
1.3	A typology of problems, power and authority	22
2.1	Partnership drivers, forms, leadership attributes and challenges	32
2.2	Towards 'collaborative thuggery'	47
3.1	Competencies of political leaders	75
4.1	The Stacey (1999) matrix developed by Zimmerman et al (1998)	81
4.2	Congruence of big and little windows: vertical and horizontal dimensions	83
4.3	The basic forms of social organisation	94
4.4	Ritual forms associated with each basic form of authority	95

Boxes

0.1	Partnership working as a matter of life or death	xi
0.2	Partnership working in everyday health and social care practice	xiii
0.3	The series at a glance	xvi
1.1	Barriers to collaboration in health and social care	5
1.2	Characteristics of boundary spanners	7
1.3	Ten principles for 'reinventing government'	13
1.4	Network forms and management styles	20
2.1	Somerset Mental Health Partnership	38
2.2	Action Zones	42
2.3	Local strategic partnerships	43
2.4	Suggested characteristics of the networker	49
2.5	Partnership life cycle	53
3.1	Weick's seven properties of sense making	68
3.2	Key messages about partnership leaders and sense making	71
4.1	Quantitative organisational culture measures	87
4.2	Crucial factors in the merger experience	88
4.3	The Somerset JCB	98

Acknowledgements

Edward and Helen would like to acknowledge the frequent discussions and previous publications with Deborah Davidson, Perri 6, Tim Freeman, Jon Glasby, Chris Skelcher and Stuart Copeland on which the content of this book draws. They would also like to thank Keith Grint (Figure 1.3), Siv Vangen and Chris Huxham (Figure 2.2), Brenda Zimmerman and colleagues (Figure 4.1), Mark Exworthy and Martin Powell (Figure 4.2) for allowing them to reproduce their work.

List of abbreviations

Health and social care use a large number of abbreviations and acronyms. Some of the more popular terms used in this book are set out below:

CCT	Compulsory competitive tendering
JCB	Joint commissioning board
JCC	Joint consultative committee
LSP	Local strategic partnership
NDIT	Neo-Durkheimian institutional theory
NPM	New public management
OECD	Organisation for Economic Co-operation and Development
PCT	Primary care trust

All web references in the following text were correct at the time of printing.

Preface

Open almost any newspaper and issues of partnership working (or lack of it) leap out at you. In extreme cases it is very rare, high-profile, front-page stories – about a child death, a mental health homicide, the abuse of a person with learning difficulties or an older person dying at home alone (see Box 0.1). Here, partnership working is quite literally a matter of life and death, and a failure to collaborate can have the most serious consequences for all involved. However, most newspaper stories focusing on social issues or on public services will inevitably include reference to partnership issues – either to the need for joint working or to a social problem that is so multifaceted that an interagency response is required. Whether it be gun crime, substance misuse, prostitution, social exclusion, regeneration, third world debt, teenage pregnancy or public health, the issues at stake are often so complex that no one agency working by itself could ever hope to provide a definitive solution (or even understand the problem in its entirety).

Box 0.1: Partnership working as a matter of life or death

Following the death of Victoria Climbié in 2000, a series of reforms have taken place in children's services to promote more effective partnerships. As the then Health Secretary explained, 'there were failures at every level and by every organisation which came into contact with Victoria Climbié. Victoria needed services that worked together. Instead the [inquiry] report says there was confusion and conflict. The only sure-fire way to break down the barriers between these services is to break down these barriers altogether' (BBC, 2003).

In services for people with learning difficulties, an investigation into alleged abuse in Cornwall found that 'working relationships between the [NHS] trust and Cornwall County Council had been poor for a considerable time' and that 'social services had little involvement in the care provided by the trust, to the detriment of people with learning disabilities' (Healthcare Commission/CSCI, 2006, p 7).

In mental health services, a review of mental health homicides identified a lack of partnership working as a common feature of official inquiries (and the fourth most important out of 12 contributing factors), both in health and social care, as well as with the police, housing and the independent sector (McCulloch and Parker, 2004).

In older people's services, 'thousands of people die miserable deaths alone, uncared for and in poverty, figures suggest. A study by Liberal Democrat MP Paul Burstow found around 60 people a week die alone without the support of family and friends' (BBC, 2005). In the MP's report, factors contributing to such isolation and loneliness were thought to include bereavement, illness, physical impairment, fears for personal safety, declining self-esteem, depression, retirement and a reduction in social participation, poverty and a lack of preventative health and social services (Burstow, 2005). These findings have since been re-iterated in a report commissioned by the Department of Health and Comic Relief (O'Keeffe et al, 2007), which found that, despite references to 'partnership' in a number of policy documents, abuse and neglect of older people remains prevalent in the UK.

In the health and social care trade press, interagency issues are even more prevalent (see Box 0.2 for examples). For health and social care practitioners, if you are to make a positive and practical difference to service users and patients most of the issues you face will involve working with other professions and other organisations. For public service managers, partnership working is likely to occupy an increasing amount of your time and your budget, and arguably requires different skills and approaches to those prioritised in traditional single agency training and development courses. For social policy students and policy makers, many of the issues you study and/or try to resolve inevitably involve multiple professions and multiple organisations – in both health and social care, and in the public, private and voluntary sectors. Put simply, people do not live their lives according to the categories we create in our welfare services (and in subsequent professional training and organisational structures) – real-life problems are nearly always messier, more complex, harder to define and more difficult to resolve than this.

Box 0.2: Partnership working in everyday health and social care practice

At the time of writing, the latest edition of *Community Care* magazine contained news items, opinion pieces and features about:

- child poverty and well-being
- a child death and allegations of insufficient interagency communication
- poor integration of services for children and/or young people
- the experience of people with learning difficulties in the criminal justice system
- services for children whose parents have a substance misuse problem.

Nursing Times contained pieces on:

- the link between mental health and substance misuse
- the education of nurses working in nursing homes
- the physical health of people with mental health problems
- joint working between the National Health Service (NHS) and the private sector to improve access to healthcare
- new ways of working to provide surgery and diagnostics in community settings.

In addition, *The Guardian* contained stories about:

- the link between substance misuse and crime
- gun crime in inner-city areas
- policies to tackle traffic congestion in busy cities
- the potential privatisation of the probation service
- parental mental health and the impact on children.

Policy context

In response, national and local policy increasingly calls for enhanced and more effective partnership working as a potential solution. While such calls for more joint working can be inconsistent, grudgingly made and/or overly aspirational, the fact remains that collaboration between different professions and different organisations is increasingly seen as the norm (rather than as an exception to the rule). With most new funding and most new policy initiatives, there is usually a requirement that local agencies work together to bid for new resources or to deliver the required service, and various Acts of Parliament place statutory duties of partnership on a range of public bodies. As an example of the growing importance of partnership working, the word 'partnership' was recorded 6,197 times in 1999 in official parliamentary records, compared to just 38 times in 1989 (Jupp, 2000, p 7). When we repeated this exercise for the publication of this book series, we found that there were 17,912 parliamentary references to 'partnership' in 2006 alone (although this falls to 11,319 when you remove references to legislation on civil partnerships that was being debated at the time) (for further details see www.publications.parliament.uk/pa/cm/cmhansrd.htm).

In 1998, the Department of Health issued a consultation document on future relationships between health and social care. Entitled *Partnership in action*, the document proposed various ways of promoting more effective partnerships, basing these on a scathing but extremely accurate critique of single agency ways of working (DH, 1998, p 3):

> All too often when people have complex needs spanning both health and social care good quality services are sacrificed for sterile arguments about boundaries. When this happens people, often the most vulnerable in our society ... and those who care for them find themselves in the no man's land between health and social services. This is not what people want or need. It places the needs of the organisation above the needs of the people they are there to serve. It is poor

organisation, poor practice, poor use of taxpayers' money
– it is unacceptable.

Whatever you might think about subsequent policy and practice, the fact that a government document sets out such a strongly worded statement of its beliefs and guiding principles is extremely important. In fact, there is often reason to question whether current commitments to the principle of partnership working are really as benign and well meaning as this quote implies. Like any significant change in policy emphasis and focus, the current trend towards closer joint working is probably the result of multiple interrelated factors (and many of these are explored throughout this current book series). However, the fact remains that partnership working is no longer an option (if it ever was), but a core part of all public services and all public service professions.

Aim and ethos of the 'Better partnership working' series

Against this background, this book (and the overall series of which it is part) aims to provide an introduction to partnership working via a series of accessible 'how to' books (see Box 0.3). Designed to be short and easy to use, they are nevertheless evidence-based and theoretically robust. A key aim is to provide *rigour and relevance* via books that:

- offer some practical support to those working with other agencies and professions and provide some helpful frameworks with which to make sense of the complexity that partnership working entails;
- summarise current policy and research in a detailed but accessible manner;
- provide practical but also evidence-based recommendations for policy and practice.

> **Box 0.3: The series at a glance**
>
> - *Partnership working in health and social care* (Jon Glasby and Helen Dickinson)
> - *Managing and leading in inter-agency settings* (Edward Peck and Helen Dickinson)
> - *Interprofessional education and training* (John Carpenter and Helen Dickinson)
> - *Working in teams* (Kim Jelphs and Helen Dickinson)
> - *Evaluating outcomes in health and social care* (Helen Dickinson)

While each book is cross-referenced with others in the series, each is designed to act as a standalone text with all you need to know as a student, a practitioner, a manager or a policy maker to make sense of the difficulties inherent in partnership working. In particular, the series aims to provide some practical examples to illustrate the more theoretical knowledge of social policy students, and some theoretical material to help make sense of the practical experiences and frustrations of frontline workers and managers.

Although there is a substantial and growing literature on partnership working (see, for example, Hudson, 2000; Payne, 2000; Rummery and Glendinning, 2000; Balloch and Taylor, 2001; 6 et al, 2002; Glendinning et al, 2002a; Sullivan and Skelcher, 2002; Barrett et al, 2005), most current books are either broad edited collections, very theoretical books inaccessible for students and practitioners, or texts focusing on partnership working for specific user groups. Where more practical, accessible and general texts exist, these typically lack any real depth or evidence base – in many ways little more than partnership 'cookbooks' that give you apparently simple instructions that are meant to lead to the perfect and desired outcome. In practice, anyone who has studied or worked in health and social care knows that partnership working can be both frustrating and messy – even if you follow the so-called 'rules', then the end result is often hard to predict, ambiguous and likely to provoke different reactions from different agencies and professions. In contrast, this book series seeks to offer a more 'warts and all' approach to the topic, acknowledging the practice realities that practitioners, managers and policy makers face in the real world.

Wherever possible the series focuses on key concepts, themes and frameworks rather than on the specifics of current policy and current organisational structures (which inevitably change frequently). As a result the series will hopefully be of use to readers in all four countries of the UK. That said, where structures and key policies have to be mentioned, they will typically be those in place in England. While the focus of the series is on public sector health and social care, it is important to note from the outset that current policy and practice also emphasises a range of additional partnerships and relationships, including:

- broader partnerships (for example with services such as transport and leisure in adult services and with education and youth justice in children's services);
- collaboration not just between services, but also between professionals and people who use services;
- relationships between the public, private and voluntary sectors.

As a result, many of the frameworks and concepts in each book (although summarised here in a public sector health and social care context) will also be relevant to a broader range of practitioners, students, services and service users.

Ultimately, the current emphasis on partnership working means that everything about public services – their organisation and culture, professional education and training, inspection and quality assurance – will have to change. Against this background, we hope that this series of books is a contribution, however small, to these changes.

Jon Glasby and Helen Dickinson, Series Editors
Health Services Management Centre, School of Public Policy,
University of Birmingham

1

What are management and leadership and why do they matter in partnerships?

Over the past century ideas derived from management, and more recently leadership, have become ubiquitous concepts in our everyday lives. There are countless books and articles about organisations that deal directly with these issues. Flick through any paper, or watch any TV channel, and they underpin discussions of responsibility and accountability that are consistent threads through many news stories. When an organisation – or groups in society more broadly – encounters difficulty, it almost invariably looks towards some form of individual leadership to guide it through the time of turbulence or to take the blame for failing to do so. Typically, media and public attention focuses on the person at the top, who is presumed to have both the authority and the acumen to intervene to make things better. As has been argued elsewhere, 'the "organisation in our heads" is still heavily influenced by the principles of classical management theory' (Anderson-Wallace, 2005, p 171), which assumes hierarchical relationships between members of a single organisation.

This deep-seated perspective on organisational life has two major implications for the consideration of management and leadership in partnership settings. Firstly, in the creation and maintenance of collaboration between independent agencies, it has privileged the importance of senior managers *within* the organisations forming partnerships, rather than those individuals developing the relationships *between* partners (although the literature on 'boundary spanners' – of which more later – has attempted to balance this tendency). Secondly, it creates an environment where there exists a strong pre-disposition, in particular in public services, to turn effective interorganisational partnerships into a new form of hierarchy (and again, this is a theme to which we will return). In these circumstances, being the manager responsible for the initiation and/or sustenance of a partnership arrangement (whether a clinical network, a joint or integrated team, a shared governance arrangement and so on) which involves the voluntary cooperation of a number of agencies and/or individuals can be a challenging position (for a more detailed discussion on these points, see Williams, 2002).

Furthermore, as noted in the Preface, the number and range of public sector partnerships has grown considerably since the mid-1990s. At the same time, the expectation that they will enable public services (and their voluntary and private sector partners) to better address the 'wicked' problems of society has also become commonplace, and, as suggested in Box 0.1, 'better' partnership working has also frequently been suggested as a way of preventing avoidable deaths and improving the quality of lives for vulnerable individuals and their families. These expectations are frequently as much aspirational as plausible. This is understandable. Politicians and policy makers usually want to persuade the public – and the latter often want to be persuaded – that new innovations in public services will deal with complex, troubling and perhaps irresolvable social problems (for further examination of this important theme, see Hoggett, 2006). Stern and Green (2005) describe what could reasonably be called a spirit of collusive over-optimism that infuses many local agency descriptions of their partnerships. Sullivan et al (2004) suggest that 'the need to justify their existence to unpredictable national funders means that localities have become adept at laying claim to impacts in all sorts of areas' (p 1610).

Readers of the entire series of which this text is a part will note that this book stands out as slightly distinct from the others. This is not simply a quirk of this book, but a result of the nature of the evidence base that the book draws on. As the introductory text to this series (*Partnership working in health and social care*, by Jon Glasby and Helen Dickinson) suggests, there are no easy answers when it comes to partnership, especially as the evidence base is drawn from a range of different disciplines and theories. In this case, the pattern is compounded further by the nature of management and leadership studies. Despite management and leadership being possibly some of the most written about phenomena of the past 50 years, the evidence base is far from conclusive and the evidence relating to management and leadership within interagency settings is complex, contradictory in places, under-theorised in some areas and theoretically dense in others. We have tried to draw out the most useful aspects of this evidence and present it in a way that is as accessible as possible for manager, practitioner and student audiences alike. However, we acknowledge this means that at times the concepts explored are challenging, but the intention is that this more nuanced account will more accurately reflect the myriad of situations that leaders and managers of partnerships find themselves encountering.

This chapter starts by considering why management and leadership issues have gained such prominence within the partnership literature, before going on to consider a certain set of individuals (commonly known as boundary spanners) who have become central within these debates. The chapter then outlines the many forms that partnerships may take and the implications this has for discussions of management and leadership of interagency initiatives. The following section provides an overview of the paradigm of new public management (NPM), the influence this has had on public policy over the past 30 years and implications for readers of this book. One consequence of NPM has been increased interest in networks and the link between partnerships and networks is considered here. The final section then moves on to consider current major theories of management and leadership in order to provide some clarity about the nature of management and leadership in partnerships.

Why is collaboration not always successful?

In the introductory text in this series, Glasby and Dickinson (2008) noted that there is little evidence that partnerships have unequivocally demonstrated improvements in outcomes for those who use services

–

(and this theme is further explored in another text in this series by Helen Dickinson, *Evaluating outcomes in health and social care*). Similarly, research from the commercial sector suggests that over 60% of alliances fail or are plagued by under-performance (Ettore, 2000), and the overwhelming message from the commercial sector literature is that mergers and acquisitions rarely succeed in delivering anywhere near the promised payoffs (for a recent review, see Field and Peck, 2003). Writing about her understanding of the North American private sector, Kanter (1989) suggests that a failure to adequately manage partnerships might be responsible for this situation. She points to research indicating that while managers spend up to 50% of their time initiating partnerships and a further 23% of their time developing strategic partnership plans, they spend only 8% of their time actually managing partnerships.

As Kanter notes, the challenge of leading and managing interagency partnerships is a more difficult task than operating in traditional hierarchical organisations where, she argues, the former may: lack a common framework between partners; exhibit asymmetrical power relations (that is, one partner holds more power than other[s]); possess incompatible values; have unclear authority and communication channels; and deploy different professional discourses. Of course, these latter three characteristics, at least, may also be present in well-established and apparently hierarchical public service organisations (such as NHS mental health trusts; see Norman and Peck, 1999; Peck and Norman, 1999). Nonetheless, Kanter's analysis does start to map out the contours of the particular terrain that has to be negotiated by those managing and leading in interagency settings.

Echoing some of Kanter's themes, UK health and social care partnerships have tended to bring together organisations which are characterised by different accountability regimes, priorities, values, institutional rules, roles and rituals, diverse financial cycles and so on. As long ago as the early 1990s Hardy et al (1992) produced a list of barriers to collaboration between health and social care that still resonate today (see Box 1.1), despite this analysis being based on relationships in place before the introduction of either the purchaser–provider split or extensive private sector involvement in healthcare. Again, this list may contain items that could also characterise individual organisations (for example, fragmentation of responsibilities within agency boundaries and professional self-interest); nonetheless, there are themes here to which we need to return in considering the particular challenges of managing and leading in interagency settings.

Box 1.1: Barriers to collaboration in health and social care

Structural
- Fragmentation of service responsibilities across interagency boundaries
- Fragmentation of service responsibilities within agency boundaries
- Interorganisational complexity
- Non-coterminosity of boundaries

Procedural
- Differences in planning horizons and cycles
- Differences in budgetary cycles and procedures

Financial
- Differences in funding mechanisms and bases
- Differences in the stocks and flows of resources

Professional
- Differences in ideologies and values
- Professional self-interest
- Threats to job security
- Conflicting views about user interests and roles

Status and legitimacy
- Organisational self-interest
- Concern for threats to autonomy and domain
- Differences in legitimacy between elected and appointed agencies

Source: Hardy et al (1992)

Evidence for the positive impact of partnerships, then, is scarce (for a thorough review, see Dowling et al, 2004) and the accounts of challenges plentiful (for example, Huxham and MacDonald, 1992; Cameron and Lart, 2003; Coulson, 2005). Rather than deploying systematic interventions to overcome these difficulties, which may take considerable senior management time and attention, agencies involved in partnerships have typically used the appointment of individual managers – network coordinators, integrated service managers, joint commissioning managers – to glue these entities together. It is presumed that these post holders will solve the problems created by these obstacles when they can (and negotiate a way around them when they cannot). As McCray and Ward (2003) suggest, partnership working is all too often 'the action of a few individuals with vision that have created change in service delivery in relation to people's lives and opportunities. These individuals have managed to work and lead effectively despite the maze of separate service budgets, distinct disciplines and different values' (p 362). In other words, in everyday practice, individual managers – and their leadership skills – are viewed as essential in making partnerships work (to the extent that they can or do work). In the broader organisational literature, these individuals are usually known as boundary spanners.

Boundary spanners

Steadman (1992) defines boundary spanners as 'positions that link two or more systems whose goals and expectations are at least partially conflicting' (p 75). Noble and Jones (2006) suggest boundary spanners are different from project champions, as they are more intimately concerned with the day-to-day machinations of a partnership, rather than simply 'cheering from the sidelines'. Project champions and senior managers create the conditions within which boundary-spanning managers must work. These individuals go by a number of different names within the literature such as *reticulists* (Friend et al, 1974), *strategic brokers* (Craig, 2004) and *entrepreneurs of power* (Degeling, 1995).

Although the next chapter provides a much longer discussion of the research on leadership and boundary spanning, it is important to establish the basic aspects of the concept here first. Williams (2002) identifies six strands in the literature on boundary spanners. Again, it is important to note that some, if not all, of the characteristics identified by Williams as common to boundary spanners might also be recognised as fundamental in all organisational managers (in particular in the more 'transformational' and 'post-transformational' models of leadership that have emerged over the past decade; see below for further discussion). However, as with the literature on the particular problems in partnerships discussed above, they may help further characterise the specific issues that need to be explored in establishing effective management and leadership interventions in interagency settings. Williams' strands are illustrated in Box 1.2, along with the sorts of skills and attributes that Sullivan and Skelcher (2002, p 101) suggest are typical of boundary spanners.

Box 1.2: Characteristics of boundary spanners

The boundary spanner as reticulist
A reticulist shows networking skills and emphasises the importance of cultivating interpersonal relationships, communication, political skills and an appreciation of the interdependencies around the structure of problems and their potential solutions. Effective networking enables a boundary spanner to understand how other actors define this phenomenon in relation to their own values and interests and this is the basis for successful negotiation.

The boundary spanner as entrepreneur and innovator
The entrepreneurial and innovative capacities of boundary spanners highlight flexibility, lateral thinking and rule breaking. Another version of this view sees them as skilled at connecting problems, policies and politics.

The boundary spanner and otherness

On this account, boundary spanners are characterised by an ability to engage with others and deploy effective relational and interpersonal competencies. This is motivated by a need to acquire an understanding of people and organisations outside their own circles – to acknowledge and value difference in terms of culture, mind-set, profession and role etc.

The boundary spanner and trust

Trust is often isolated as one of the most important factors to influence the course of interorganisational relations. Various models of trust implicate the concept with faith, predictability, goodwill and risk taking; boundary spanners need to be both aware of the importance of trust and be adept in its generation.

The boundary spanner and personality

The literature is peppered with innumerable references to the personalities, character, traits and disposition of boundary spanners. There are suggestions that they are personable, respectful, reliable, tolerant, diplomatic, caring and committed, to name but a few. The proposition is that good collaborative behaviour is a function of particular personal attributes.

Source: Adapted from Williams (2002)

- Critical appreciation of environment and problems/ opportunities presented
- Understanding different organisational contexts
- Knowing the role and playing it
- Communication
- Prescience
- Networking
- Negotiating
- Conflict resolution
- Risk taking
- Problem solving
- Self-management

Source: From Sullivan and Skelcher (2002)

Partnership form and implications for management and leadership

Of course, also crucial to the formulation of the most effective form of management and leadership is the nature of the partnership within which it is being exercised. There are numerous frameworks that seek to categorise partnerships (Hudson et al, 1998; Leutz, 1999; Ling, 2002) but perhaps the most helpful in this context is the depth/breadth matrix (Peck, 2002) and a version of this was also introduced in the introductory text in this series (Glasby and Dickinson, 2008). This invites partners to consider the balance they are aiming to strike between the depth and breadth of their relationship (see Figure 1.1).

Figure 1.1: Depth versus breadth of relationship

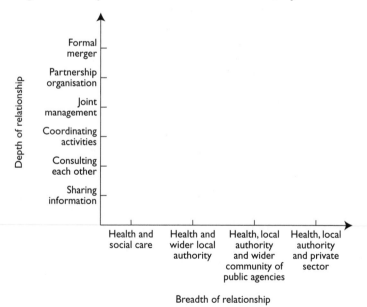

There are a number of brief points to make about this framework:

- Firstly, it should be seen as representing the dynamic nature of partnerships, reflecting that they have the potential to re-position themselves over time and do not just exist in a static form. For example, the creation of a care trust − a formal merger of health and social care − may well follow periods of coordination and joint management (see Glasby and Peck, 2003; Glasby and Dickinson, 2008).

- Secondly, it raises the question of whether health and social care communities can pursue breadth and depth simultaneously. In other words, does the creation of a health and social care merger serve to reduce the potential for partnership with other agencies, at least in the short to medium term? (For an example that seems to illustrate this tendency, see Dickinson et al, 2007.)

- Thirdly, it can accommodate partnerships around commissioning as much as those around providing, where it is important to acknowledge that the former may be as significant in health and social care as the latter (see below for further discussion of the role of commissioning).

- Fourthly, it can also encompass public relationships with the private sector, whether these are commissioner−provider (based around information sharing about need and demand) or provider−provider (such as the formal partnership organisation constituted by a joint venture).

- Finally, and linked to these last two points, it also enables incorporation of the three ways of thinking about organisational relationships which are fundamental to one of the most influential frameworks, that is, hierarchies, markets and networks.

As discussed in Glasby and Dickinson in this series (2008), a hierarchy is a single organisation with top-down rules, procedures and statutes that govern how the organisation works. Such organisational forms have tended to dominate public services; even where markets and networks have become more prominent in recent years, they are typically new ways of handling relationships between hierarchies. In a study of the prevalence of collaborative public management in the US, McGuire (2006) notes: '[F]ar from being episodic or occurring in just a few programmes, collaboration in public management is as common as managing bureaucracies, and even more so in such areas as economic and community development, the environment, energy management, and the entire gamut of social and human services. It is important to recognise that bureaucracy is not going away; collaboration still complements, rather than supplants, single organisation and management' (p 40).

In contrast, a market involves multiple organisations exchanging goods and services based on competition and price. A network is often seen as lying in between these two approaches, with multiple organisations coming together sometimes more informally and perhaps voluntarily, often based on interpersonal relationships or shared outlooks or outcomes (Thompson, 1991; 6 et al, 2006). Rodríguez et al (2007) have caricatured these approaches as being about: rules (hierarchy), incentives (market) and interactions (network). In discussing health and social care partnerships, therefore, we are looking at various forms of networks; however, some of these partnerships may increasingly be made obligatory (think of youth offender teams) or encouraged to transform into new forms of hierarchy (think of community mental health teams) or asked to operate in a market (think of joint commissioning boards [JCBs]) (for a more detailed discussion, see Glasby and Dickinson, 2008).

New public management

Some commentators have identified these organisational forms with specific periods of recent history: 1940s–1970s, hierarchy; 1980–1990s, markets; and post-1997, networks. Although misleading in some respects, this approach links discussions of networks to one of the most important ideas in organisational writing over the past two decades: new public management (NPM). We will give a short overview of NPM at this point because of its importance to the prevalence of, and enthusiasm for, networks (and also for the popularity of the division in public services of commissioning from providing which has accompanied the trend towards networks).

In 1995, the Organisation for Economic Co-operation and Development (OECD) observed that 'a new paradigm for public management has emerged, aimed at fostering a performance-oriented culture in a less centralised public sector' (1995, p 8). Essentially NPM is founded on a critique of hierarchy as the organising principle of public administration (Dunleavy, 1991); it is argued that the top-down decision-making processes associated with this model are increasingly distant from the expectations of citizens. The case went that, while the commercial sector had undergone radical change in the 1980s, the public sector remained 'rigid and bureaucratic, expensive, and inefficient' (Pierre and Peters, 2000, p 5). This explains why NPM is often seen as the application of private sector management techniques to the public sector. Of course, many in the public sector have stressed the significant differences between the two sectors and thus the inappropriateness of such an application (for example, Carnevale, 2003). In an interesting – and research-based in as far as the studies are robust – refutation of this position, Boyne (2002) argues that only three of thirteen hypotheses about such differences seem to be borne out in practice: 'public organisations are more bureaucratic, and public managers are less materialistic and have weaker organisational commitment than their private sector counterparts' (p 98).

Various advocates differ in their descriptions of NPM (Pollitt, 1993; Hood, 1995; Ferlie et al, 1996). In general, however, it is characterised as an approach which:

- emphasises establishment and measurement of objectives and outcomes;
- disaggregates traditional bureaucratic organisations and decentralises management authority;
- introduces market and quasi-market mechanisms;
- strives for customer-oriented services.

Osborne and Gaebler's (1993) popular text *Reinventing government* is a prominent example of the NPM paradigm. It sets out 10 main principles for reforming the public sector in order that it might become more aligned with a commercial sector ethos (see Box 1.3).

Adopting these principles also contains implications in the way that public sector organisations are managed and led. Indeed, the benefits of NPM are often described in contrast to the drawbacks of 'old public administration' where the latter is said to be characterised as the diplomatic maintenance of organisations that are inward looking and which have been designed and are run in the interests of the professional staff who work in them (Harrison et al, 1992). From another perspective, Lynn (2006) describes this approach as being 'governed by rules and hierarchy, and by the public service values of reliability, consistency, predictability, and accountability' (p 142). NPM, on the other hand, favours managers and leaders who are, for instance, customer-focused and entrepreneurial. Of course, this is an over-simplistic dichotomy; nonetheless, in these circumstances, the enthusiasm for the transformational model of leadership in public services since the late 1990s (see below) is easier to understand.

Box 1.3: Ten principles for 'reinventing government'

1. *Catalytic government:* steering, not rowing
2. *Community-owned government:* empowering rather than serving
3. *Competitive government:* injecting competition into service delivery
4. *Mission-driven government:* transforming rule-driven organisations
5. *Results-orientated government:* funding outcomes, not inputs
6. *Customer-driven government:* meeting the needs of the customer, not the bureaucracy
7. *Enterprising government:* earning rather than spending
8. *Anticipatory government:* prevention rather than cure
9. *Decentralised government:* from hierarchy to participation and teamwork
10. *Market-orientated government:* leveraging change through the market

Source: Osborne and Gaebler (1993)

As Lawler (2000) describes, the introduction of new managerialism stressed 'the role, power and accountability of individual managers and accentuates their positions as managers, rather than as administrators, officers or senior professionals. Accountability for success or otherwise lies at the door of each individual manager, operating within strategic guidelines and being responsible for the achievement of organisational objectives' (p 33). Growing pressures for economic and social change in the 1990s, and the election of a government in 1997 which had distinct ambitions in terms of public sector reform, saw interest in the management of public services being superseded by a focus on 'highly effective leadership and a requirement for new leadership skills' (PIU, 2001, p 11). Davidson and Peck (2005, pp 43-4) note that up until the late 1990s, the word 'leadership' appeared infrequently in healthcare policy pronouncements, whereas between 1998 and 2001 it featured in over 70 Department of Health documents and circulars. We return later in this chapter to this differentiation between management and leadership.

Many of the major reforms of health and social care over the past 25 years can trace their roots back, at least in part, to ideas derived from NPM; from the introduction of general management in the NHS and compulsory competitive tendering (CCT) of goods and services, which up to this point were provided by local authorities in the 1980s, through to the purchaser–provider splits of the 1990s, to the plurality and choice agenda of the 21st century. For our present purposes, one of the key consequences of NPM needs highlighting, which is connected to the first of Osborne and Gaebler's principles (Box 1.3): *governments should steer, but not row*. Underpinning this tenet is the argument that if public sector bodies concentrate on *what* should be delivered (and the performance management of outcomes), then they will do so more efficiently if they are not preoccupied with the details of *how* this should be delivered.

Implications of NPM for public sector management and leadership

Over the past 25 years, therefore, many public services have ceased to be provided by the NHS and local authorities (or by government more widely) and have been transferred to a wide variety of agencies (for example, private companies providing domiciliary care, voluntary bodies proving community-based drug and alcohol services, arm's length maintenance organisations providing housing services, foundation NHS trusts providing mental healthcare). This has led to a proliferation of providers, many of which are markedly different in their origins, incentives and governance arrangements (and we shall return to the topic of governance in Chapter 3). Not for nothing have commentators described the emergence of the 'congested state' (Skelcher, 2000) during the 1990s, where an increased number of organisations now need to collaborate in order to address the 'wicked' problems of society exemplified in the Preface to this book.

Of course, it would be misrepresenting history to argue that there was no plurality in the sources of public service provision prior to NPM (we need only remember primary care and residential care to refute that position). Nonetheless, successive UK governments came to realise that 'wicked' problems require (almost by definition) collaboration across agencies, and consequently the number of agencies that need to be involved in such collaboration increased. The current emphasis on partnership working between health and social care is, therefore, in no small part, a consequence of the extensive influence of NPM.

Furthermore, 'steering' in health and social care has come to mean commissioning. NHS and local authorities divesting themselves over time of provision – the rowing – has had two immediate results:

- Firstly, partnerships have had to take place at – and between – two levels: commissioning organisations (primary care trusts [PCTs] and local authorities) and providing organisations. No longer is the collaboration largely between two predominant hierarchical bureaucracies that combine responsibility both for strategic planning (*what*) and operational management (*how*), as was the case pre-1989 (albeit that neither PCTs nor local authorities are yet entirely free from aspects of direct provision).

• Secondly, partnership has been pursued since 2000 in a policy environment that has encouraged contestability as much as collaboration which has left some managers and leaders – in particular in commissioning organisations – puzzling over the appropriate local balance in a context where the political messages over support for competition can be mixed (Field and Peck, 2003; Freeman and Peck, 2007).

In due course, it may be that even commissioning is seen as another form of rowing. The further extension of practice-based commissioning and the energetic implementation of direct payments and individual budgets could put significant amounts of commissioning responsibility and resources in the hands of private agencies and individual citizens. This would both necessitate a whole new set of commissioning partnerships and a re-orientation of PCTs and local authorities into the sorts of strategic activities that are becoming associated with a concept known as 'place making'; for this reason Chapter 3 contains a section focused on leadership and place making.

Partnerships and networks

Because of a tendency to use words such as 'partnership' indiscriminately to refer to a range of ways of organising, it is helpful to return to the framework of hierarchies, markets and networks. Thus, as the depth/ breadth matrix helps reveal, many current health and social care 'partnerships' have now become hierarchies. Equally, some market-based relationships – for example, many public–private partnerships – are misleadingly described as 'partnerships', partly, perhaps, because they can involve long-term relationships, but mostly because use of this term may be politically more acceptable. In this book, therefore, the focus is on managing and leading in and around agencies attempting to collaborate within genuine networks. The definition of partnership developed by Armistead et al (2007) is also useful here: 'a cross-sector, cross-organisational group, working together under some form of recognised governance, towards common goals which would be extremely difficult, if not impossible, to achieve if tackled by a single organisation' (p 212).

This clarification raises another important way of sharpening our focus. By examining the literature on networks, it may be possible to further develop characteristics of managing and leading in interagency settings. The good news is that this literature is enormous and the bad news is … this literature is enormous. One attempt at classifying types of networks suggested by 6 et al (2006) is presented in a simplified form in Table 1.1. This typology suggests that there are at least seven distinct sets of drivers for the creation of networks. Of course these drivers may overlap in specific cases or, indeed, come into conflict (for example, when different motives are driving partners). Where drivers come into conflict it may be the case that not all these drivers can be successfully incorporated into any one composite network form. That is, when it comes to network drivers, not all good things can go together (see Chapter 2 for more detailed discussion).

Furthermore, the identification of these seven sets of drivers also suggests that the influence of individual or collective approaches to management and leadership may vary significantly between various forms of network (for example, this influence can be predicted to be much greater in personal networks than in those driven by technological innovations). In addition, it may be worth considering whether in any collaboration the espoused reasons for pursuing partnership (such as those in public consultation documents) tell the whole story of the drivers in play (for an interesting discussion of this topic in relation to NHS trust mergers, see Fulop et al, 2005). Many of these kinds of documents major on the drivers of *organisational competence* and/or *problem contingency*, when the timing and design of the network may be as much shaped by the financial and institutional context (that is, although it is often suggested that changes are an attempt to address certain issues, they may in fact also be driven by financial factors or due to other wider political or cultural pressures). It is also worth bearing in mind that prevailing political or organisational fashion may be a significant factor in the forms that local partnerships take (see, for example, Peck and 6, 2006).

Table 1.1: A classification of types of networks

Theory	Driving force shaping networks	Distinct form of networks based on
Resource exchange/financial (in particular reducing transaction costs)	Focus on securing and optimising efficient use of resources (and minimisation of transaction costs)	*Content*, that is, the nature of the resources – money, staff – exchanged
Organisational competence and learning	Focus on securing new competencies and knowledge (and maximisation of benefits)	*Content*, that is the competencies and knowledge desired
Personal	Focus on connections between individuals (and thus organisations)	*Structure*, or the overall pattern formed by these personal connections
Institutional	Focus on patterns of established authority, accountability and procedures in organisations joining network	*Institution*, with each example shaped by the local interaction of these patterns
Ecological	Focus on organisational interests in forming clusters to exploit specific resources in particular niches	*Content*, that is, the nature of the niche to be exploited
Problem/technology contingency	Focus on solving particular problems	*Institution*, with each example shaped by the nature of the problem and the potential solution
Macro-economic/technological determinist	Focus on the consequences of technology available to solve problems	*Content*, with each example shaped by the nature of and innovations in technology

Source: Adapted from 6 et al (2006)

Drawing on neo–Durkheimian institutional theory (NDIT) (of which more in Chapter 4), 6 et al (2006) go on to suggest that another way of conceptualising networks is to link them to four basic ways of organising which are present in all organisations (see Figure 1.2). According to this framework, organisations can be classified according to the way that they predominantly organise themselves; as a consequence, there

Figure 1.2: Conceptualising networks around four basic ways of organising

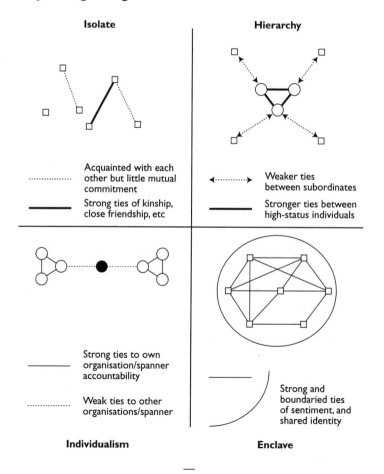

is a form of network that they will favour. These four forms differ from each other in terms of the sorts of behaviours and styles of sense making that are important (and Chapter 3 explores the issue of sense making in more detail).

In reality, individual organisations exhibit a combination of – also known as a 'settlement' between – these ways of organising. When agencies work in partnership with other organisations each individual partner is obliged to seek a compromise between its preferred way of organising and those of it partners. At this stage, it is important to note that this theory suggests that by determining the characteristics of partnerships in terms of these ways of organising, managers and leaders may be able to behave in ways that are more harmonious with the prevailing settlement (Box 1.4 clarifies this with examples). In other words, if leaders and managers can act in ways that are consistent with

Box 1.4: Network forms and management styles

- A manager in a *hierarchical network* will have authority derived from their position and will achieve impact by calling on the formal rules and roles of the partnership.
- A manager in an *enclave network* will get their authority from commitment to the cause and achieve impact by appealing to the shared goals of the partnership.
- A manager in an *individualistic network* will get their authority by an ability to connect disparate organisations and individuals and achieve impact by the outputs and outcomes that these alignments can deliver.
- A manager in an *isolate network* – something of a contradiction in terms – will struggle to gain authority or achieve impact but may do so through the power of personal relationships.

It is important to note that most networks will actually be hybrids which combine elements of all of these four ways of organising and managers will need to be able judge the most appropriate interventions for the hybrid in which they are operating.

the form of settlement then they may find that their actions are more acceptable and accepted by individuals and organisations (and this is congruent with ideas articulated in situational theories of leadership outlined below).

Theories of management and leadership

So far, this discussion has tried to introduce some of the complexities related to notions of health and social care partnerships and to clarify some of the characteristics that may help describe the specific challenges of, and approaches to, managing within them. We shall use these challenges and approaches to construct a framework to give structure to the discussion of research evidence in Chapter 2. The remainder of this chapter explores some of the current major ideas around management and leadership. Unfortunately, these theories are as complex in nature as the issues surrounding partnership. In seeking clarity about the nature of management and leadership in partnerships, the definition offered by O'Leary et al (2006) of collaborative public management may be helpful. They argue that it is '[A] concept that describes the process of facilitating and operating in multiorganisational arrangements to solve problems that cannot be solved or easily solved by single organisations. Collaborative means co-labour, to cooperate to achieve common goals, working across boundaries in multisector relationships' (p 7).

To date, we have used management and leadership interchangeably; however, much of the literature proclaims that there is a clear distinction to be made. Where leaders are transformational, managers are transactional (Zaleznik, 1992; Dubrin, 2004). The former do the right thing while the latter merely do the thing right (Bennis, 1994). Perhaps the most helpful distinction for our present purposes is articulated by Grint (2005b). He argues that the distinction between management and leadership is best understood through an analysis of the problem to be solved (wicked, tame or critical) and the nature of the power to be exercised (hard power or soft power) (see Figure 1.3).

In his framework:

- *Critical problems* require an immediate intervention with hard power and therefore demand a command response (where the priority is to provide an answer).
- *Tame problems* are ones that organisations have seen before and thus have an established reaction, and require a managerial response (where the priority is to organise a process).
- *Wicked problems* are the sort that health and social care partnerships are established to address and require a leadership response that deploys soft power (where the priority is to ask questions).

There is potential compatibility between transaction and organising processes, and transformation and asking questions. Nonetheless, Grint is careful not to make extravagant claims on behalf of leaders (and he has a very particular perspective on the role of leaders in posing these questions to which we shall come back shortly).

Figure 1.3: A typology of problems, power and authority

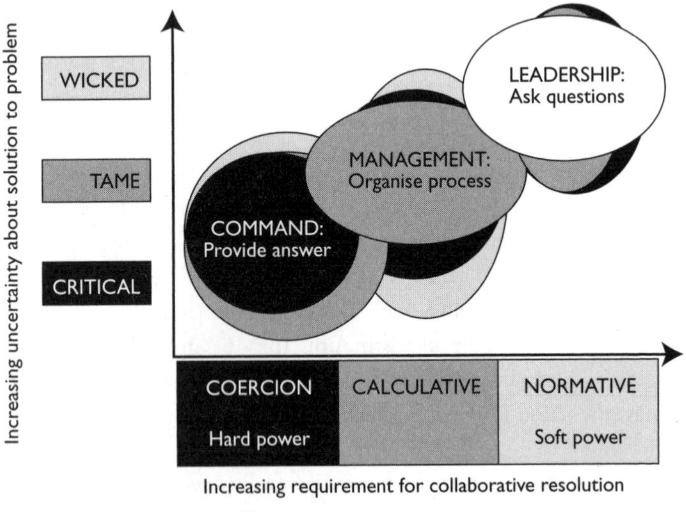

Source: From Grint (2005a, p 1477)

In contrast to those who would make a firm distinction between leadership and management, Pye (2005) suggests that 'it seems much less significant when what really matters is (effective) organising' (p 35). This seems to us both an insightful and pragmatic observation. As a consequence, we will use leadership from here on to represent *those activities that might enable effective organising, especially within partnerships.* A more interesting question might be to ponder why New Labour has championed leadership to such a significant extent (see, for example, PIU, 2001). Perhaps part of the answer lies in the foreword to a later document from the Scottish Executive (2005) that argues: 'leadership is not a peripheral issue; it is central to improving performance, redesigning services and securing better delivery' (p 1). Investment in leadership is, therefore, an intervention in health and social care that will support the implementation of the reform agenda of government. In these circumstances, as has been argued at greater length elsewhere (for example, Blackler, 2006; Peck and 6, 2006), what the New Labour government considers effective leadership starts to look suspiciously like smart followership.

Leadership is possibly one of the most researched topics of the past 50 years. Yet it remains a contested topic (as the last two paragraphs illustrate), under-theorised and reliant on a few popular views and perspectives (Bolden and Gosling, 2006). Alvesson and Svengisson (2003) suggest that this lack of a universal definition may be helpful; they argue that a single definition of leadership is not practically possible (given the range of different ways that the term has been employed) and, even if it was, might hinder the growth of new ways of thinking about leadership which do not conform to the established definition. At the same time, there is a relatively sparse amount of literature that directly considers management and leadership within partnership settings (to which we will return in the next chapter). Against this background, we will briefly explore the wider management and leadership literature to illuminate some of the key theories and perspectives surrounding leadership, and also consider the different skills and competencies which leadership in partnership settings may require in comparison to more traditional models. Drawing on Peck (2006, pp 323-41), we can identify six broad models of leadership that, while they have broadly emerged sequentially, still remain influential in the literature today. These are summarised, along with their implications for leadership development interventions, in Table 1.2.

Table 1.2: Summary of major approaches to leadership

Approach	Emphasis	Development implications	
Great man	Personal traits	Few – leaders are born, not made	
Situational/personal–situational	Context dependence	Can develop the interpersonal to some degree, but mostly developing use of different approaches in certain contexts	
Psychological profiling	Psychological traits	Limited development of the interpersonal	Time
Behavioural	Actions appropriate to followership	Development of the intrapersonal	
Transformational	Relationship between leader and followers	Development of the inter and intrapersonal	
Post-transformational	Sense making	Development of the inter and intrapersonal	

Much of the early leadership literature at the start of the 20th century initially focused on the leadership of 'great men'. This regards the innate characteristics of the individual as imperative, with context having little influence. According to this perspective, leaders are born. Although certain aspects of leaders may be developed through training programmes, it is unlikely that someone who is not born with these 'great man' traits will be able to be developed into a leader. The remnants of trait theory can be seen in accounts of both transformational leaders (for example, charisma) and boundary spanners (for example, creativity), although these are arguably moving more towards a 'great woman' theory of leadership. In health and social care settings, the 'great man' approach seems alive and kicking, particularly among politicians. For example, it is evident in New Labour's proposal for management 'franchising' in healthcare, where a chief executive apparently successful in one organisation would be given responsibility for another that is perceived to be failing.

In contrast to trait theorists, the *situational* approach suggests that leadership styles have to be adopted as a response to the demands of a given situation; contextual factors thus determine who emerges as a leader. In time, this led to the evolution of *personal–situational* theories. These maintain that, in any given case of leadership, some aspects are due to the situation, some result from the person and yet others are consequent on the combination of the two (Bass, 1960). This way of thinking established that there was a crucial relationship between context and leadership that was to prove increasingly influential and, indeed, still shapes many leadership development programmes delivered today.

After the Second World War, writers developed notions of leadership based on a number of factors which, again, put the individual centre stage: the interrelations between individuals (Likert, 1961); individual motivation (Maslow, 1954); the interdependence between individuals and organisations (Blake and Moulton, 1965); and the fit between individual and organisational needs (McGregor, 1966). These writers established the importance of the individual's *psychological profile* to leadership, representing in some ways the return of a more sophisticated form of trait theory. Perhaps the best known psychological inventory – the Myers Briggs Type Inventory – was initially put together by psychologists in the 1940s (Briggs Myers, 2000) and is still widely used in leadership development programmes. These writers also set the stage for the entrance of concepts which are also now commonplace, for example, 'emotional intelligence' (that is, an ability to perceive, assess or manage the emotions of an individual's self and of others) (Salovey and Mayer, 1990; Goleman, 1996). George (2000) stresses the importance of four aspects of emotional intelligence to leadership: the appraisal and expression of emotion, the use of emotion to enhance decision making, knowledge about emotions and the management of emotions. These theorists, with their stress on the importance of the personal resources of the individual, found their ideas very much back

—

in favour when the solutions to the problems of late 20th-century corporations was seen as lying in the capabilities of chief executives (Storey, 2004b).

During roughly the same period, a number of accounts took further the idea that the interaction between the person and the situation was of paramount importance, and also started to raise the profile of followers. *Path-goal theory* (House, 1971) suggested that successful leaders show their follower the rewards that are available and the paths (that is, the behaviours) through which these rewards may be obtained (and this seems to have resonance with the approach adopted towards health and social care by the Department of Health three decades later in the notion of 'earned autonomy'; see below). *Contingency theory* (Fiedler, 1967) argued, rather simplistically, that leaders have a tendency towards either task-orientation or relation-oriented leadership (that is, leaders either focus on tasks or on relationships). Later, Vroom and colleagues (Vroom and Yetton, 1973; Vroom and Jago, 1988) elaborated this theory by postulating that three factors influence the choice of leadership style:

- the degree of structuring of the problem
- the amount of information available
- the quality of decision required.

Hersey and Blanchard (1988) added as an additional variable the readiness of followers to accept leadership. While sharing the limitations of other theories in this tradition – for example, paying no regard to the constraints imposed on leaders by the pre-existing patterns of authority, accountability and procedures within organisations (Giddens, 1993) – the suggestion that leaders can identify (and indeed, in the argument of Grint, 2005a) factors that might influence their selection of leadership style has become important.

Before *transformational leadership* made its entrance on to the theoretical stage in the 1990s, it was preceded by charismatic leadership. In many respects, this signalled a return to the certainties of the 'great man' era. Perhaps best seen as one, and only one, characteristic of transformational leaders – a necessary but not a sufficient condition –

the charisma of chief executives was a cause for celebration in the 1980s (for example, Peters and Waterman, 1982) and a cause for concern 20 years later (Mangham, 2004). Perhaps the most considered overview of this theory is provided by Bryman (1992). Although many writers (for example, Bass, 1990) have given sober accounts of the attributes of transformational leaders towards their followers – for example, individualised consideration, intellectual stimulation, inspirational motivation and idealised influence (that is, providing a role model) – others can look aspirational and, on occasions, fanciful (for example, Alimo-Metcalfe, 1998; Boje and Dennehey, 1999, respectively). Nonetheless, the transformational trope can draw attention to two often overlooked aspects of leadership (both of which are highlighted by Grint, 2005b). Firstly, the identity of a leader – charismatic or otherwise – is relational rather than individual. That is, 'leadership is a function of a community not a result derived from an individual deemed to be objectively superhuman' (Grint, 2005b, p 2). Secondly, leadership has to be embodied: 'leadership is essentially hybrid in nature – it comprises humans, clothes, adornments, technologies, cultures, rules and so on' (Grint, 2005b, p 2), that is, it has to be performed. This latter dimension of leadership is becoming increasingly important and is the subject of a separate section in Chapter 3.

Finally, there are also signs of some new trends emerging; these seem to suggest a number of directions that have not yet coalesced into a 'school' (which is presumably why Storey, 2004c, gives them the name 'post-transformational'). The most important of these focuses on leadership as sense making (see Chapter 3 for more discussion of this concept). Fullan (2001) draws on the seminal work of Weick (for example, 1995) who provides an accessible introduction to the notion of sense making: 'Active agents construct … events. They "structure the unknown"…. How they construct what they construct, why, and with what effects are the central questions for people interested in sensemaking' (p 4). As Weick puts it, 'sensemaking is about authoring as well reading' (p 7); for him, it involves creation as much as discovery. The importance of Weick's work here is that it emphasises the potential for changing the way in which organisational pasts, presents and futures

—

are constructed by organisational members and, in particular, by the interventions of organisational leaders.

Fullan (2001) identifies five independent but mutually reinforcing components of effective leadership:

- moral purpose
- understanding the change process
- relationship building
- knowledge creation and sharing
- coherence making.

The focus on this last element – leaders as sense makers – is central to recent papers on leadership by Grint (for example, 2005a; and Pye, 2005) – where the purpose of leaders asking questions is to enable consensual construction of the nature of the problem. There are also a range of theories that can broadly be described as theorising 'distributed leadership' that, it is argued, may be particularly relevant to partnerships. These include ideas around informal leaders (Hosking, 1988), decentred leadership (Martin, 1992) and shared leadership (Judge and Ryman, 2001). While these accounts are not always entirely clear about what is being distributed (and by whom) – or whether it is being actively distributed or merely taken – they do acknowledge the organisational reality of the power of what elsewhere have been termed 'street-level bureaucrats' (Lipsky, 1980). This refers to the ability of frontline professionals to organise local procedures and practices to suit their own interests (although the date of Lipsky's study suggests that this tendency may not be especially limited to partnerships).

This chapter has provided much food for thought on the subjects of partnership, leadership and the relationship between them. However, most of this material has been prescriptive (saying how things ought to be) rather than analytical (reflecting on research undertaken in the field). In the following chapter we move on to this descriptive literature, using key themes from this chapter to organise the various studies into a coherent framework. In so doing, we focus on the leadership of networks – collaborative partnerships between agencies – rather than hierarchies (such as care trusts) or contractual relationships formed in a market that aim to address predominantly tame problems (and thus specify timescales and outputs at the outset). This will hopefully enable us to zoom in on those aspects of leadership that are especially important to partnerships.

Reflective exercises

1. What do the terms 'leadership' and 'management' mean to you? Share your perspectives with a colleague from a different professional or organisational background and compare and contrast your different definitions.

2. In what ways do you think the leadership and management of partnerships are similar to and different from that of 'traditional' hierarchical organisations?

3. Think of the different forms which health and social care partnerships might take and consider which modes of leadership (based on Figure 1.2) might be appropriate in each.

4. Think of an effective leader you have encountered. What were the particular qualities or actions of this individual that made you respect this person?

5. Think of an individual you have encountered in your professional or private life who you would describe as a boundary spanner. What makes this individual a boundary spanner? What skills or attributes does this individual possess which you think makes them suitable for this role?

Further reading and resources

For an overview of how public leadership is conceptualised by central government and the importance it holds, see the Performance and Innovation Unit's review of leadership (2001) *Strengthening leadership in the public sector.*

For a useful introduction to leadership theory see Grint's (2005b) *Leadership: Limits and possibilities.*

For an introduction to partnership theory in the private sector see Kanter's (1994) 'Collaborative advantage' in *Harvard Business Review.*

For an overview of NPM see McLaughlin et al's (2002) *The new public management.*

Useful websites for leaders and managers include:

- British Academy of Management: www.bam.ac.uk
- The Community Leadership Association: www.communityleadership. org
- Lead International Incorporated: www.lead.org/
- Chartered Management Institute: www.managers.org.uk

2

What does research tell us?

Taken together, the various frameworks examined in Chapter 1 suggest that there are:

- distinct sorts of drivers for, and thus forms of, partnership;
- a set of traits, behaviours and skills attributable to leaders that might enable partnerships to function better;
- a range of apparently predictable challenges that partnerships might face.

The first task of this chapter, then, is to bring these three elements together into one overarching framework (see Figure 2.1). The second is to explore whether there is research evidence which supports and enriches this framework.

Reflecting on Figure 2.1, certain correlations start to suggest themselves. While it would be difficult to express all these in a two-dimensional format, it may be worth drawing one or two for the purposes of illustration. For example, it could be hypothesised that a network established to exchange resources would struggle with a lack of a shared framework and may prioritise predictability among its leadership. On the other hand, a network set up to exploit a specific niche may be undermined by complexity of accountability and communication and would prioritise entrepreneurialism in its leaders. Thus, Figure 2.1 may in itself prove to be a useful analytical tool for those involved in network leadership. However, a couple of caveats are necessary:

- Firstly, partnerships are typically driven by *more than one aim* (and these aims may be difficult to achieve simultaneously).
- Secondly, agencies engaging in partnerships *may have divergent drivers* (and their public motives may differ from their private ones).

Figure 2.1: Partnership drivers, forms, leadership attributes and challenges

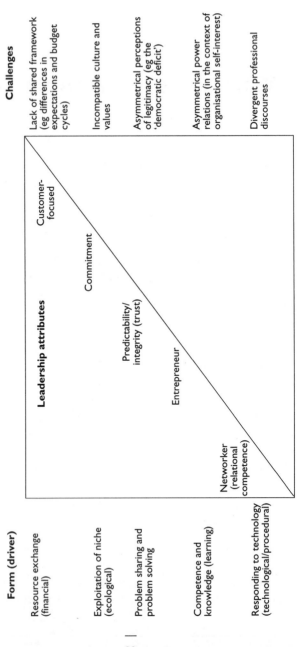

- Thirdly, the *attribution of leadership* should not be taken as being synonymous with the traits, behaviours and skills of one individual leader; indeed, it would be someone with a very wide repertoire that could exhibit all of the attributes in Figure 2.1 (and we shall return in Chapter 4 to the virtues of 'requisite variety' when considering ways of organising).

Furthermore, a number of the challenges – such as some aspects of the lack of shared framework – may be beyond the reach of any local leadership to overcome. As a consequence, we must be cautious in not imbuing leadership with ambitions that are simply unrealistic. We shall return in Chapter 3 to the idea of leadership as performance – and the limitations within this – but at this stage it is sufficient to note that at least part of the trajectory followed by any partnership will be determined by the patterns of authority, accountability and procedure that carry weight in the agencies that join and the interaction between them (this is the institutional element contained in Table 1.1).

Is leadership 'the answer'?

It is important to recall that in the previous chapter we suggested that leadership has been viewed as one way in which health and social care organisations might be 'glued together'; at a local level, therefore, leadership can be assumed to be responsible for part of the way in which that partnership develops. As evidence of this, Mitchell and Shortell (2000, p 242) suggest that problems associated with governance and management of community health partnerships are possible reasons why they have not demonstrated significant, measurable outcomes. Further, in a study of the US health sector, Weiss et al (2002) identify leadership as the most significant factor in stimulating synergy in partnerships; in this context, synergy is described in terms of the ability to enable partners to think in new and different ways in order to achieve their goals. Leadership is also singled out as the key factor in a Health Action Zone project (see below) in Northern Ireland (Rugkåsa et al, 2007).

—

Thus, leadership is often identified retrospectively as being a key factor in the success or otherwise of partnerships. In the case of personalistic networks (again, see Table 1.1), where the interactions of organisations are regarded as the consequence of relationships between individuals, the space for management and leadership to exert influence may be presumed to be at its most potent. However, it is our view that this personal element should be seen as representing one of the potential facets of leadership – the *networker* showing *relational competence*, for instance – rather than as a distinct form of network in its own right. This is on the basis that any network purely rooted in individual contacts that did not connect with the broader aspirations of the organisations concerned – such as the need to pursue *problem sharing and problem solving* – would only either serve the interests of the individuals concerned and/or be short-lived (and there is evidence for this from recent studies of Health Action Zones; see Barnes et al, 2004).

Perhaps, again, therefore we should be a little cautious here about the enthusiasm of some research for the leader as key variable in leadership success; rather, the question should be not 'did leadership lead to the success of this partnership' but 'how big a part does leadership really play in the trajectory of effective partnerships?'. Pollitt (2000) notes that within the history of the NHS there is something of an uncritical, acceptance and implementation of the latest simple prescription for improvement; in recent years, this has undoubtedly included transformational leadership (for example, Bevan, 2005). Lawler (2004) suggests the assumption is often made that leadership is desirable, that people will welcome it and that it is necessarily unequivocally a 'good thing'. As a consequence, it is frequently identified as a crucial factor within the literature. This reinforces Gemmill and Oakley's (1992) argument that leadership might, in fact, be a 'social fiction', that is, because leadership is increasingly seen as unquestionably crucial to effective organisations, then one of the causal factors of effective organisations must be leadership.

Consequently, commentators may tend to attribute a number of changes or outcomes to leadership when they may in fact have been influenced by other factors. Jim Collins (2001) suggests this reflects a tendency to view 'leadership as the answer to everything', which is the modern equivalent of the 'God is the answer to everything' perspective that 'held back our scientific understanding of the physical world in the dark ages. In the 1500s, people ascribed all events they didn't understand to God. Every time we attribute everything to leadership we are no different from the people in the 1500s. We're simply admitting our ignorance' (pp 21-2). This is a strong statement, but one that is worth bearing in mind in what follows; Collins is arguing that in our enthusiasm for leadership we may well be overlooking other important causal factors when considering the success (or, indeed, failure) of partnerships.

Finally, we cannot simply presume that leadership always has positive impacts (see Mangham, 2004). O'Toole and Meier (2004) investigate what they call the 'dark side' of network management and suggest that there are some potentially negative impacts which might flow from these processes (particularly relating to benefits accruing around certain groups and not others); it may be that Vangen and Huxham (2003) are referring to such consequences arising from the 'collaborative thuggery' that we discuss below.

What does the evidence say about managing and leading partnerships?

The literature relating to leading (and managing) in interagency settings is limited in terms of scope, focus and consistency. Yet despite this, much of the literature relating to theories of interagency collaboration still make bold claims about the role of leaders in managing sets of complex organisational, structural and cultural factors. This chapter reviews the claims made for leadership within interagency settings and questions the extent to which they are evidence based. For example, many of the claims made for the boundary-spanning roles pertain to transformational models of leaders as charismatic individuals; is there robust evidence for the efficacy of this style or, in practice, does interagency leadership relate more to shared *leadership* than to

—

traditional models of the individual *leader*? This is a question to which we shall return.

Furthermore, when interagency leadership is featured in research, it is frequently presented in contrast to that within 'traditional' organisations (for example, Sullivan and Skelcher, 2002; McCallin, 2003; Goldsmith and Eggers, 2004). Table 2.1 represents one such example of the genre. While not unhelpful, it does seem a little naïve in its presentation of the 'classical' perspective. In our experience of health and social care, many of the challenges within single organisations require the 'network' perspective; in some ways such approaches merely serve to present the over-simplistic transactional/transformational dichotomy in a new guise.

Table 2.1: 'Classical' and network management compared

Perspective dimensions	'Classical' perspective	Network perspective
Organisational setting	Single authority structure	Divided authority structure
Goal structure	Activities are guided by clear goals and well-defined problems	Various and challenging definitions of problems and goals
Role of manager	System controller	Mediator, process manager, network builder
Management tasks	Planning and guiding organisational processes	Guiding interactions and providing opportunities
Management activities	Planning, designing, leading	Guiding interactions and providing opportunities

Source: From Kickert et al (1997)

In the course of the following discussion we summarise the research literature that relates specifically to networks. First, we consider the implications for leadership of the different forms of partnership, using the five forms identified in Figure 2.1 to structure the material. Subsequently, we explore evidence on what leaders are thought to bring to interagency settings and the roles which research suggests they actually achieve – or the issues they have the ability to influence – in practice. In this discussion we deploy the five leadership attributes

—

from Figure 2.1. Where some immediate overlap between these two perspectives is apparent then it is highlighted.

Different network forms: their characteristics, difficulties and outcomes

The discussion of forms of partnership presented here draws in part on the work of 6 et al (2006). Overall, they note, the general findings of Bass' (1974) review of the leadership literature are no doubt relevant to interorganisational contexts. That is, effective leaders need to achieve network centrality, establish areas of influence and span structural 'holes' regardless of the particular form of the network. However, as noted in Chapter 1, one fruitful way to think about leadership is to look at the structural position of leaders in their personal networks. That is, to consider their role in organisational networks from the viewpoint of the interaction between their personal networks and the interorganisational structure (or form). This suggests that we should look at leaders in the present context as 'boundary spanners'.

Resource exchange networks

Thompson (1967) presented a model of the organisation as consisting of a core of activities, the boundaries of which are buffered by certain functions which protect the integrity of the core, but are also spanned by certain categories of role holders charged with bringing in certain resources (or taking them out). This is predominantly a *resource exchange* model (many studies privilege this approach as economists have been very active in the network literature). These roles may be involved in both shielding the core from external threats and in bridging to external opportunities. Overall, what distinguishes *resource exchange networks* is that, as 6 et al (2006) summarise, they can be defensive – 'interorganisational forms are driven by factors that are predominantly negative, that is by the pressure to reduce such costs and by the imperative to avoid failures in transactions' (p 16) – or more positive – 'based around the tendency of individuals or organisations to pursue

—

both competitive and comparative advantage and therefore market power. They do so by configuring their tangible and intangible assets, skills, resources and relationships in order to optimise their benefits' (p 16). Note that, in both cases, the organisational motivations are essentially self-interested.

Thompson (1967) also distinguished between cases in which the boundary-spanning function worked to highly prescribed rules on transactions with external organisations (*predictability*) and those where the boundary spanners have discretion (*entrepreneur*). Examples from commercial organisations which stress *predictability* – and are thus perhaps more defensive in orientation – would include account managers who are responsible for managing downstream vertical ties with customers and purchasing and procurement managers charged with handling upstream vertical ties along the supply chain (Katz and Kahn, 1966). There are also accounts of boundary spanners who are more *entrepreneurs*, responsible for horizontal network maintenance, because they are charged with liaising with particular interorganisational groups, representing the organisation externally, or forming coalitions (see Aldrich and Herker, 1977); this clearly is the more positive mode. In the latter case, we are also moving towards the *ecological* perspective on networks to which we turn shortly.

Box 2.1 presents examples of resource exchange networks. The first demonstrates an example of cost reduction due to this form, while the second, although overtly stating to be driven by a need to improve services, implicitly appeared to be related to resource exchange.

Box 2.1: Somerset Mental Health Partnership

Provan and Milward (1995; Milward and Provan, 2000) found that a highly structured, integrated and regulated network form in mental health services seemed to be effective in controlling transaction costs of purchasing, contracting and compliance. In common with many innovations in partnership over the past 10 years, the creation of the Somerset Partnership Mental Health and Social Care NHS Trust was predominantly described locally

---

as an approach driven by *learning* and *problem sharing and problem solving*. However, it became clear during the evaluation of the impact of this merger (Peck et al, 2002b) that there was also an expectation that the new partnership arrangement would ease local financial pressures (which turned out to be unfounded; see Peck and 6, 2006).

Networks that exploit niche

In the later development of Thompson's population ecology (*exploitation of niche*) theories of organisational fields (for example, Aldrich, 1979), boundary-spanning roles and activities came to be seen as functions that were critical not only both to the structure and competence of each organisation but also to the structure of the whole organisational field (and their collaboration). In order to exploit a specific niche, or indeed to realise the benefits of other drivers, the presence of individuals in different agencies in whom the responsibility for interorganisational relationships is vested is important to the development of partnerships; a lone boundary spanner is lonely indeed. More recently, Takeishi (2001) argues that 'both practitioners and strategy researchers have paid increasing attention to networking, alliances, and cooperative inter-firm relations ... researchers have argued that firms with collaborative inter-firm relations could be more competitive than those without' (p 404). This suggests that boundary spanners can play an important role in creating an environment where new initiatives – such as joint ventures between public and private agencies – may become more likely. In this, the most market-orientated of the five forms, the individualist way of organising identified by 6 et al (2006; see Figure 1.2), is clearly the most pronounced.

It is this theoretical context – somewhere between positive notions of *resource exchange* and the joint ventures of the *ecological* perspective – that ideas around collaborative advantage, championed by Huxham and her colleagues in public sector partnerships (for example, 1996) come into play. The term seems to originate with Kanter (1994), again looking at partnerships in the US, but also Asian and European private sectors, from which she identified three characteristics of

---

partnerships which participants viewed as crucial to their success. Firstly, they must yield benefits that go beyond the immediate deal, that is, 'beyond the immediate reasons they have for entering into a relationship, the connection offers the partners an option on the future, opening new doors and new opportunities' (p 97). The presence of such anticipated benefits also seems to us like one criterion which serves to differentiate networks from contracts. Secondly, effective partnerships 'involve *collaboration* (creating new value together) rather than mere *exchange* (getting something back for what you put in' (p 97; original emphasis). Thirdly, 'they cannot be "controlled" by formal systems but require a dense web of interpersonal connections' (p 97). These characteristics seem most pertinent to a joint venture which 'might operate independently or it might link the partners' operations' (p 98); this latter description could be seen to accurately describe the aspirations of a range of health and social partnerships.

Of course, not all networks created to share resources in order to exploit specific niches are completely successful. Integrated healthcare networks in the US have pursued vertical integration (that is, integration between specialist or acute care and community or primary care services) but this has in some cases served to increase costs and produce uneven profitability. There have been limits on the extent to which integration in financial planning could be achieved, and differences in organisational culture between agencies involved remain important (Bellandi, 1999; Lin and Wan, 2001; Wan et al, 2001).

Huxham (for example, Vangen and Huxham, 2003) picks up on this point, contrasting the optimism of collaborative advantage with the wide experience of collaborative inertia: 'the often-pertaining actual outcome, in which the collaboration makes only hard fought or negligible progress' (p 62). In particular, this aspect of her work looks at the leadership challenges within collaborations, sharing our reluctance to differentiate between leadership and management and arguing – in keeping with the institutional tradition summarised in Figure 1.2 that was also developed in Chapter 1 – that 'structure and ... processes ... are as instrumental in leading to a collaboration's outcomes as is the behaviour of the participants associated with it' (p 62).

—

Problem-sharing and problem-solving networks

It is the perceived 'wicked' issues that face society that drive many partnerships in health and social care (and, indeed, the broader networks represented in Figure 1.1).

> On this view, the structures and capabilities of different forms of inter-organisational relations are shaped most by the prevailing technologies of production that require (or do not require) particular inter-organisational links with other organisations possessing access to other specific technologies. The argument suggests that once the nature of the task and the nature of the technologies necessary for undertaking that task have been established, then the structure, form of accountability and efficacy of the network forms that will most suit those conditions can, at least in principle, be identified. (6 et al, 2006, pp 18-19)

These *problem-sharing and problem-solving networks* have been extensively researched through the example of Health Action Zones, area-based initiatives that sought multiagency bids from health and local authorities to address specific local problems. As 6 et al (2006) also note, the assumed fit between the nature of the problems and the choice of the partnership form to address them is not typically borne out in experience. Boxes 2.2 and 2.3 present examples of *problem-sharing and problem-solving partnerships* and the lessons about leadership and management that they suggest.

The Somerset study (Peck et al, 2002b; see also Box 2.1) raises two further interesting questions regarding *problem sharing* and *problem solving*. Firstly, it concludes that 'the establishment of the combined Trust did not – at the conclusion of the evaluation period – appear to have delivered significant benefits that have not been delivered elsewhere in England without the transfer of social care staff to NHS employment' (p 40). In other words, the adoption of the specific partnership approach was not essential to the sharing and solving of the problem (in this case, enhanced professional coordination in service delivery). Secondly, the problem shared and solved between the hierarchies of the NHS and local authority had no impact on the problems perceived by the clients of the service as priorities that, after three years of merger, were as pressing as ever. This suggests that *customer focus*, while important in the prescriptions for attributes of network leaders, may not appear very strongly in the empirical literature.

Box 2.2: Action Zones

One of the most significant innovations in government-sponsored partnership working was the creation of Action Zones (covering health, education and employment) during New Labour's first term (for an overview, see Powell and Moon, 2001). Promising additional resources and some non-specific relaxation of rules of engagement, localities were awarded Zone status following a competitive process (one local authority – Plymouth – was successful in achieving all three).

Interestingly, the extensive national evaluation of Health Action Zones re-confirms many of the challenges earlier identified, and adds some new ones (for example, the problems of engaging voluntary and community groups; see Matka et al, 2002) and says little about the nature of leadership in these partnerships.

In the final report on the development of collaborative capacity (Barnes et al, 2004), the researchers do note, however, that: 'the pressures and conflicting priorities sometimes faced by "middle managers" need to be acknowledged, and these players need to be empowered to act in ways that will enhance collaboration rather than otherwise' (p 63). This suggests that the most intractable organisational obstacles that partnership leaders may face do not lie in either senior executives or frontline professionals; they argue that it is in the middle manager tier that 'the tension between innovation and meeting performance targets can be acute' (p 64). They also observe that committed individuals are crucial and agencies need to invest in the development of such capacity.

—

Box 2.3: Local strategic partnerships

The national evaluation of local strategic partnerships (LSPs), an ongoing initiative that developed further the aspirations that underpinned Action Zones, contains a specific paper on leadership issues (ODPM, 2005b). These nationally prescribed arrangements, initially established to respond to share and solve overall problems defined by government which were reflected in a significant list of centrally imposed targets, bring together health, local authority and the wider community of public, voluntary and commercial agencies (that is, they are the furthest point on the breadth axis in Figure 1.1).

It identifies three stages to partnership – dialogue, strategy formation and delivery – and three parallel fields of leadership: political leadership (discussed further below), which supplies democratic legitimacy and the resources and power of the local authority; leadership from partner organisations; and leadership within the community (and this theme is picked up in a section on leadership and place in Chapter 4; see Rugkåsa et al, 2007, for an account of boundary spanners working 'downwards'), which means securing the consent and active engagement of the wider community.

It may be that in seeking for unique features of leading in partnerships that this idea of boundary spanners working simultaneously across three apparently distinct ways of organising may be useful.

Learning networks

Of course, *learning* is also a key driver of these large public sector partnerships. On this account, 6 et al (2006) argue that:

> ... agencies are presumed to make astute and intelligent judgements of the competence requirements of their field, the links they will seek to form with other firms will be ones that

enable them to enhance their own core competencies. Such
links will seek to generate efficient and effective divisions of
labour between partners in order to secure the competencies
and capabilities that the firms do not have the ability, need
or wish to cultivate internally. (p 17)

In a recent study of regeneration partnerships, Hemphill et al (2006)
found that 'one of the recurring responses centred on the collective
learning and associated benefits that the members felt they gained from
being part of a multisector partnership' (p 75). Davies (2004) suggests
that a habit of partnership working can be generated which fosters an
almost ideological commitment to collaboration, which then results in
more partnership activity. This is an interesting suggestion that *learning*
can apply to the process of doing partnership – and lead to a tendency
to see more of it as the solution to all sorts of challenges, as perhaps
occurred in Somerset (Peck et al, 2002b) – and not just the content
of the original partnership.

The literature suggests that, although information-sharing networks
are often best driven by their members (see 6 et al, 2006), this does not
necessarily make them easy to maintain. Sermeus et al (2001) examine
the network of hospitals known as the Belgian-Dutch Clinical Pathway
Network, where membership had to be sustained by continuous efforts
in persuasion. Similarly, a study on Project CHAIN (Community
Health Alliances through Integrated Networks), a university-supported
information network around improving quality of life for older people
in South Wales (Warner et al, 2003), suggests that, without mandatory
membership and lacking any well pre-defined output, even developing
protocols for coordination in community-based medication required
extensive work to stabilise the membership and negotiate with
powerful and sometimes mutually suspicious professions (and these
studies suggest that *commitment* may well be a key characteristic of
some effective network leaders).

In the English NHS, numerous 'collaboratives' have been established
by the Department of Health between different organisations over
the past 10 years in order to facilitate service improvement. However,
it has transpired that this model is vulnerable in several key respects.

Bate and Robert (2002) conclude that these networks were too bureaucratic in their design, not enabling communities of practice to arise which would have been more adept at sharing tacit knowledge (that is, in the terms of the framework introduced in Figure 1.2, they privileged the hierarchical way of organising over the enclave). McLeod (2005) points to 'the consequences of the model's short timescale, explicitly aiming to promote change rapidly by attempting to create the initial "tension for change" (or "tipping point") without recourse to potentially time-consuming activity to establish "proof" of the need for change' (p 264). Overall, these 'collaboratives' seem to have been designed and delivered to predominantly focus on *problem sharing and problem solving* rather than *learning*; once again we are alerted to the use of language by leaders – in this case in the Department of Health – for rhetorical impact (as opposed to as a plausible description of organisational arrangements).

Technology-driven networks

Technology-driven network forms are consequent, it is argued, on the forces and relationships of production. When these forces and relationships change, so do the network forms. Many of the available studies look at partnerships driven by *technology* where leadership makes a difference to the success with which interorganisational networks can operate (for example, Volkoff et al, 1999, show that the successful development of interorganisational data systems is importantly dependent on product champions working across organisational boundaries). In their study of local partnerships in US public administration involved in the joint adoption and use of geographical information systems-based technologies, Brown et al (1998) found that their measures for the presence of active leadership was a statistically significant – and positive – factor in all of their assessments of outcomes (albeit they are less clear about what sort of leadership). Fleming and Waguespack (2007) explore: 'What types of human and social capital identify the emergence of leaders of open innovation communities? Consistent with the norms of an engineering culture, we find that future leaders must first make strong technical contributions' (p 165). This suggests that, in the health and social care setting, technological innovation through networks is most appropriately led by practitioners (and this may also start to give more substance to the popular concept of distributed leadership).

However, beyond these technical contributions, they argue leaders must maintain support by:

> Two correlated but distinct social positions: social brokerage and boundary spanning between technological areas. An inherent lack of trust associated with brokerage positions can be overcome through physical interaction. Boundary spanners do not suffer this handicap and are much more likely than brokers to advance to leadership. The research separates the influence of human and social capital on promotion, and highlights previously unexamined differences between brokerage- and boundary-spanning positions. (Fleming and Waguespack, 2007, p 165)

Actually, these issues have been examined. Bardach's (1998) analysis of his case studies led him to suggest that 'effective' leadership was important for network success, both in his interviewees' estimation and in his own research evaluation. Like Fleming and Waguespack, he distinguishes between facilitative – more neutral, consensus-building – approaches and advocacy approaches that are more partisan (and which may be readier to leave people out of coalitions). Bardach is not able to demonstrate the different conditions within networks for the efficacy of using each type of his identified approaches to leadership. However, using one of the frameworks introduced in Chapter 1 (Figure 1.2), it seems plausible that advocacy styles would be more likely to be effective in individualistic or hierarchical networks and facilitative styles more likely to be seen as legitimate in enclave type networks.

Vangen and Huxham (2003) also note that the facilitative approach can co-exist with 'pragmatic approaches that, at face value, seem less consistent with the spirit of collaboration' (p 70). For instance, partnership leaders seem to take an active role in establishing the purpose of the network, that is, adopt what Bardach sees as an advocacy role, where 'power and influence can be exercised on the direction of the collaboration through definition of issues' (p 70). There are links back here to the earlier leadership model of Grint, where leaders attempt to socially construct the wicked problem to be addressed, and forward to our discussion in Chapter 4 of the importance of issue framing. This observation brings a welcome breath of reality to the discussion; as they point out, leaders of partnerships have targets to meet, especially in UK public services, and have to actively avoid perceptions of failure or inertia. It chimes with our critique in Chapter 1 of many of the features of transformational leadership being aspirational, if not fanciful, in terms of the challenges faced by public services.

Their term for this advocacy stance, rather oddly, even allowing for dramatic effect, is 'collaborative thuggery'. Its characteristics are summarised in Figure 2.2. In the more detailed discussion, it transpires that this 'thuggery' is used by partnership leaders to overcome the

Figure 2.2: Towards 'collaborative thuggery'

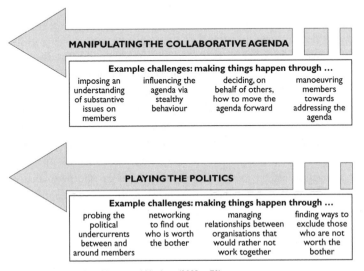

Source: Reproduced from Vangen and Huxham (2003, p 70)

sorts of challenges outlined in Figure 2.1. They conclude that leaders of partnerships need to be adept at both facilitation and 'thuggery' and at managing the interaction between them: 'an overemphasis on either would not be likely to generate collaborative advantage' (p 73); in our view boundary spanners need to be adept at both. Again, we shall return to some of these (presumably) thuggish – let us settle for the more neutral 'manipulative' – techniques in Chapter 4. With this qualification in mind, let us move on, then, to the attributes of facilitative partnership leaders.

What the evidence suggests are attributes of facilitative partnership leaders

Many of the major studies of recent years stress the elements described as *networker* (*relational competence* in Figure 2.1). Discovering that networking skills are required to lead networks may not be the biggest surprise, albeit that accounts of characteristics of networkers are not necessarily consistent across these studies. Nonetheless, many of the characteristics captured in these accounts also quite closely relate to aspects of the transformational model of leadership. One of the apparent paradoxes of these studies is that while notions of leadership in partnership seem to stress the importance of process, many of the necessary skills could be best seen as individualised traits. In other words, although this literature highlights the fact that leadership within partnership settings is shared and relational, there is still a tendency to construct lists of personal competencies that individuals should develop in order to be successful interagency leaders. Moreover, many of these characteristics also cleave quite closely to charismatic notions of leadership. This reported importance of the relational aspects of partnership leaders has prompted us to focus on the performative aspects of leadership as one of the emerging themes in Chapter 3.

Three recent papers suggest some of the characteristics of the *networker* (set out in Box 2.4). Williams (2002) concludes that 'there is a general view that the "real" business of partnership work is effected within the framework of … personal exchanges. It is where difficulties are shared, aims agreed, problems sorted out, deals struck and promises made – all out of the public gaze' (p 118). This illustrates once more the difficulties inherent in leading and managing partnerships, and also the way in which these entities often rely on personal relationships and extensive action 'backstage'.

Box 2.4: Suggested characteristics of the networker

Koppenjan and Klijn (2004) suggest collaborative managerial tasks involve:

- intervening in existing patterns of relations and restructuring relationships;
- furthering the conditions for cooperation through consensus building;
- joint problem solving.

Goldsmith and Eggers (2004) suggest that the main elements of partnership management are:

- big picture thinking;
- coaching;
- mediation;
- negotiation;
- strategic thinking;
- interpersonal communications;
- team building.

Willumsen (2006) outlines the characteristics of leadership within interprofessional collaboration as:

- facilitating interaction processes and ensuring cohesion;
- providing resources;
- encouraging interaction processes;
- relating to formal frameworks;
- dealing with everyday activities;
- establishing communication channels.

Other skills the literature (for example, Kanter, 1989; Harrigan, 1995; Child and Faulkner, 1998) suggests are required to successfully manage partnerships include:

- trust and relationship building;
- accommodating diverse values;
- having a broad strategic vision;
- network brokering;
- negotiation;
- cross-organisational communications;
- collaborative leadership styles;
- conflict resolution;
- flexibility.

The *entrepreneur* is less overtly common in the literature. Luke (1997) may be describing something similar in a discussion of catalytic leadership; that is, the ability to spark action and motivate others to take action. These individuals are also often referred to as 'champions', or as Mayo (1997) calls them, 'Godfathers'. They do not have to belong to the most obviously powerful group but have to possess sufficient personal capacity to bring people together. Sullivan and Skelcher (2002) suggest this could be a religious figure, or a business person with a particular passion for an issue in an area. Often partnership champions do tend to be associated with individuals who come across as compelling or magnetic – charisma made flesh – but as also having the authority – moral as well as organisational, perhaps – to generate multiagency interest in, and support for action around, a particular local issue. This conception of the *entrepreneur* – as champion or catalyst – may also serve to bring back to the fore that effective leadership of partnerships may be a collective rather than a personal endeavour. It would be an unusual *entrepreneur* who would want to design and deliver the detailed governance arrangements that seem to contribute to *predictability/integrity (trust)*.

This is important as one of the central themes that emerges from Armistead et al's (2007) focus groups with partnership leaders relates to *trust*. It is identified as being crucial to addressing the inherent problems of partnerships – leaders 'should be trusted' (p 222) – and *integrity* appears to have been one of the traits that participants saw as most important. Interestingly, they note that 'the predominant discourse was underlain first by "traditional" conceptions of leadership couched in terms of traits, attitudes, competences' (p 225), that is, it was conceptualised, as they acknowledge, in terms deriving from ideas around leadership in single organisations. Kanter (1994) highlights the importance of integrity – 'the partners behave towards each other in honourable ways that justify and enhance mutual trust' (p 100) – as one of the eight I's that create successful partnerships. Similarly, from their work around public partnerships in Scotland, Vangen and Huxham (2003) put 'the need to build trust' at the top of the list of activities that underpin collaboration.

As Sullivan and Skelcher (2002) note, the majority of partnerships exist as unincorporated associations; that is, health and social care partnerships often have no formal legal identity even though their constituent partners may ultimately be accountable for the services which they produce. This returns us to the point that many partnerships are essentially voluntaristic, that is, arrangements between consenting adults where members can decide, with varying degrees of free will, to walk away. It is in this context that the importance of *relational competence* and *trust* become apparent.

At the same time, continued collaboration cannot be dependent on the networking skills of an individual alone; being clear about respective partners' responsibilities, for instance, is also imperative for a partnership's internal smooth running (Wildridge et al, 2004). Rejecting the emphasis on the personal, Vangen and Huxham's (2003) theoretical stance 'conceptualizes *leadership* as the mechanisms that *make things happen in* a collaboration' (p 62; original emphasis). In the partnership 'life cycle' models that we touch on shortly, one of the stages seems to involve putting in place structures and procedures that are intended to make the partnership *predictable* for members. As an example, Chapter 3 has a section that deals in depth with the impact that formal governance arrangements have been demonstrated to have on interagency performance.

Furthermore, as the discussion of effective *learning* networks in a previous section suggests, their voluntaristic nature may require considerable *commitment* to sustain involvement. Poxton (1999) argues real success will depend to a large extent on the determination of practitioners and managers. Giving the term a slightly different connotation, the framework introduced in Figure 1.2 suggests that leadership in an enclave will necessitate the leader showing significant enthusiasm for the shared beliefs of the group. Sullivan and Skelcher (2002) review the experience of local partnerships for the promotion of coordination in activity to combat crime and social disorder in the UK over more than two decades. During the period of Conservative administrations, they show the emphasis was on largely voluntary partnerships; in such conditions, some localities achieved much through their *commitment* to their joint objectives. Barnes et al (2004) also draw attention to the evidence from Health Action Zones that: 'innovative projects require higher than usual levels of commitment and result in considerable personal investments from those involved' (p 65); they also report that: '[E]ffective collaboration requires attention to the well-being of collaborators' (p 65).

The conclusion of Boyne (2002) about the apparent lack of organisational commitment of public sector managers – in comparison to their private sector counterparts – is relevant in this context. It might be assumed that the explanation may lie in this former group of managers having more desire to serve the public interest rather than the latter, but this is not supported by Boyne's evidence (the key factor here seems to be a much more pragmatic one about the lack of a clear connection between commitment and reward). Indeed, one study (Peck and Wigg, 2002) has shown that managers in mental health services in London only expected to stay in a particular job for at most three years. In these circumstances, it is presumably all the more important that partnerships in the public sector are more institutional than personal in nature.

—

Interestingly, there is little on *customer focus* in the research literature, even in those studies based in the private sector (for example, Kanter, 1994). There are, however, some other relevant contributions that it is worth summarising here. Like the LSP review (ODPM, 2005b) discussed above, Agranoff and McGuire (2001) suggest a life cycle-type approach with four different categories for the behaviours of collaborative managers: activation, framing, mobilising and synthesising (Box 2.5).

Box 2.5: Partnership life cycle

- *Activation* involves identifying the right people and resources for the efforts of the partnership (suggestive of *entrepreneur*).
- *Framing* includes facilitating agreement on leadership and administrative roles, helping to establish a culture and helping to develop a structure (*predictability*).
- *Mobilising* is the aim of inducing enthusiasm to the collaborative and ensuring support from key external stakeholders (*commitment*).
- Finally, *synthesising* involves helping to create productive and purposeful interaction between members of the collaborative (which seems to take us again to *networker*).

In a similar fashion, Vangen and Huxham (2003) produce a four-stage model of: embracing, empowering, involving and mobilising. On careful analysis, this schema seems to have quite a lot in common with Agranoff and McGuire (2001) and again appears to create a sequence that emphasises attributes of *entrepreneur*, *predictability*, *commitment* and *networker*.

Another body of work has examined the idea that leaders of partnerships face peculiar stress arising from role ambiguity – and even conflict – because of the pressures placed on them both by their own organisation and the others with which they develop linkages (Robertson, 1995; O'Toole, 1998). Unfortunately, this research is not very extensive (although Barnes et al, 2004, also refer to this issue). It can be hypothesised that boundary spanners often exhibit ambivalence in their accountabilities because of the potential conflicts and tensions in their roles, having pressures both from their employing organisation and from the organisations with which they develop links. A linked literature (exemplified by Gould et al, 1999) argues from a systems psychodynamic perspective that attention should also be paid to the 'deeper, less conscious and more irrational processes that may infuse organizational alliances' (p 699) citing, for example, 'paranoid concerns and fantasies about the long-term lack of equity in the transfer of knowledge and capability' (p 698).

Overall, however, from their extensive consideration of leadership in networks, 6 et al (2006) conclude:

> [I]t is important to note that nothing in the boundary spanning literature shows that there is anything particularly distinctive either about the activities or about the skill sets of boundary spanners working between organisations when compared, for example, with colleagues working between departments within an organisation. Essentially, the same processes of initiation, negotiation, diplomacy, problem-solving and strategic development – and the same tact, ability to move between accountabilities, energy to motivate others etc – are required in both settings. Indeed, much of the literature moves seamlessly from the inter- to the intra-organisational context. (p 157)

This appears a slightly controversial position to adopt, albeit one that may usefully serve to demystify the concept of leadership in partnerships. There may be nothing unique to partnerships about the leadership styles and skills that facilitate their success; rather the difference may lie in the emphasis on particular elements of a more generic leadership model and in the specific contexts – and the challenges therein (see Figure 2.1) within which they are deployed.

Those that challenge the conclusion drawn by 6 and his colleagues argue that it is indeed the very nature of these contexts that differentiates leadership in partnership. Armistead et al (2007) put this point clearly:

> [C]ompared to single organizations, working in partnership
> is of an order more complex and ambiguous, wherein
> inter-organizational relationships can be horizontal as well
> as hierarchical ... without necessarily diluting hierarchy ...
> where there is uncertainty about who leads and who follows
> ... where leadership can be represented by organizations
> rather than individuals within organizations ... and where
> governance arrangements (if they exist at all) may not really
> reflect leadership as it manifests itself in practice. (p 213)

This is a persuasive argument for the network setting requiring
distinctive styles of leadership, in particular, styles that call for more
emphasis on aspects – such as *networker (relational competence)* and
commitment – that would be less prevalent in uniorganisational
arrangements. However, it must be remembered that this was not
the predominant view of the partnership leaders with which they
undertook their own research.

So, in summary, what can we take from this review of the research
evidence?

- Firstly, the evidence suggests that the five forms of network presented
  in Figure 2.1 – and their associated drivers – do seem to exist
  as broadly distinct, if interrelated, types. At the same time, some
  networks may have drivers that differ between members such that
  mismatches between aim and structure may be perceived.

- Secondly, the attributes of boundary-spanning leaders in partnerships
  are also largely vindicated, with the notable exception of *customer
  driven*, although the characteristics highlighted in each category vary
  across studies. Broadly, these four attributes are consistent with the
  transformational accounts of leadership which have predominated
  in the literature over the past 10 years.

- Thirdly, there is also an apparently helpful distinction between
  facilitative – to which the four highlighted attributes seem to
  belong – and advocacy approaches to boundary spanning which
  serves to stress that both so-called transformational and transactional

leadership approaches are relevant (that is, we should not overlook in networks the leadership styles that have been found to be prevalent in single organisations; for example, path–dependency approaches which use target setting and target monitoring). In particular, the creation and maintenance of legitimised joint mechanisms for the public discharge of authority, accountability and procedures emerges as one of the key leadership processes (in particular in cementing *predictability/integrity [trust]*).

- Fourthly, there would also seem to be evidence for the partnership life cycle that may serve to privilege certain attributes at certain times, perhaps regardless of the network form.

- Finally, there is apparent support for the suggestion that the contexts within which leadership is exercised do mean that leadership in partnerships differs in degree, if not in its fundamentals, from that within single organisations (for instance, the emphasis on *commitment*).

Reflective exercises

1. Look at a policy document extolling the virtues of public service collaboration. Try and identify which of the drivers outlined in Figure 2.1 are suggested – and which are most prominent – in this document. Do you think the drivers that you pick out really reveal the motivations of the authors?

2. Think of a partnership you have encountered or read about. What were the drivers of that partnership and what challenges has it – or do you think it may have – encountered as a result of these drivers? Which of the leadership attributes from Figure 2.1 would be most effective in this partnership?

3. Think of a situation where you believe that effective leadership was responsible for a good outcome. What was it specifically about this leadership that resulted in a positive outcome or were there any other factors which were also important? In what ways might this leadership have produced negative outcomes?

Further reading and resources

For a good introduction to issues around public policy collaboration and theoretical drivers of partnership see Sullivan and Skelcher's (2002) *Working across boundaries*. For an inclusive and detailed overview of the many forms which networks take and the implications this holds for the practice of 'networks' in the public sector see 6 et al's (2006) *Managing networks of twenty-first century organisations*.

For a review of the boundary spanning literature see Williams (2002).

There are a range of national evaluations which all make reference to leadership and management in some form including:

- Local area agreements (ODPM, 2005a, 2007)
- LSPs (ODPM, 2005c)
- Health Action Zones (Barnes et al, 2005)
- Children's Trusts (University of East Anglia, 2007)
- Health Act flexibilities (Glendinning et al, 2002a)
- National Sure Start evaluation (National Sure Start Evaluation, 2005)

For a detailed and local level study of an early and innovative partnership see Peck et al's (2002b) Somerset evaluation.

3

Hot topics and emerging issues

Through a series of themed sections, this chapter explores three current and future key issues in management and leadership in interagency partnerships:

- How do formal governance arrangements impact on the instrumental and symbolic performances of interagency collaboration and how should leaders and managers deal with these (drawing on a paper by Peck et al, 2004a)?
- Leadership as sense making and performance.
- Leadership and place making.

What do we mean by formal governance, what is the evidence and what can it do?

Discussions of 'governance' have become commonplace in health and social care over recent years and 'good governance' seems to be seen in some quarters as offering potential answers to some of the complex challenges facing public services. Indeed, for some commentators, having a form of recognised shared governance is one criterion that marks out a genuine partnership (Armistead et al, 2007). Drawing on evidence from both the private and public sector on governance, this short section explores three key interrelated questions:

- What do we mean by governance (and how does it differ from management)?
- What is the evidence on governance?
- What can good governance do?

What do we mean by governance?

Governance refers to the mechanisms that legitimise authority, accountability, policies and procedures in organisations – or in the relationships between organisations – within the social and political environment in which they operate. In the case of the networks of organisations, they serve to distribute involvement in this legitimisation around a selected range of interests. The term 'governance' has become so important over the past 10 years as a consequence, it seems, of public policies increasingly, according to Lynn et al (2001), being delivered:

> ... through complicated webs of states, regions ... nonprofit organizations, collaborations, networks, partnerships and other means for the control and coordination of dispersed activities. (p 1)

These complicated webs have to achieve public purposes in a context where traditional accountability to elected national politicians and local councillors is more and more supplemented by the likes of appointed boards, neighbourhood councils and the co-option of service users. Governance of these webs, then, is often discharged by deliberately hybrid groups drawn from all of these sources in order to give legitimacy to the oversight of a network of organisations all contributing to the local resolution or amelioration of a 'wicked' public policy problem. Partnership governance is also partially about continuing to ensure public accountability at a local level for public services delivered by these partnerships in a context where elected systems are either diminishing in influence (as is the case with local government), never existed at a local level (as in the NHS) or never existed at all (as with the private sector). When these disparate elements are brought together into partnerships they can result in a wide variety both of constitutional forms (and Sullivan and Skelcher, 2002, identify nine from their review of the literature) and assumptions about roles (more about which later).

We want to distinguish, at least in our search for a definition, this broad conception of governance from the narrower framing of corporate governance that has been highlighted in recent years by the series of corporate scandals (in both public and private sectors) that have served to underline the importance of good corporate governance. Nonetheless, the importance of effective corporate governance – and the consequences of corporate governance arrangements that are perceived as flawed – is currently on the minds of organisational officers and members. It may be that it is this context, as much as any new challenges represented by the new forms of governance that are currently emerging, that is making participants in the governance of partnership arrangements especially sensitive to issues around their authority and accountability.

What is the evidence on governance?

Given our emphasis on a broad conception of governance being distinct from the narrower idea of corporate governance, it is ironic that much of the evidence on governance derives from research on corporate boards. The research on corporate boards – the formal meetings at which corporate decisions are presumed to be made – is, at best, lukewarm about their influence in those areas, such as strategy making and monitoring, where it is typically prescribed that they should have their impact.

In the NHS, partially observation-based studies by Peck (1995) and Ferlie et al (1996) underline that there has been a gap for some time between the role prescribed by government for non-executive directors in the NHS and the apparent activities of the boards themselves. There is a similarly limited yet illuminating literature based on the observations of private sector boards. In one typical study, Winkler (1974, 1975) observed board meetings in 19 companies and noted that 'most board meetings we observed were formalistic affairs, with meagre debate, few probing questions, little serious discussion even. They were certainly not the forum in which the critical decisions of capitalism were made ... effectively, the board was a legitimising institution for decisions taken earlier and elsewhere' (1975, p 140). Many commentators have discussed the reasons for the apparently marginal impact of corporate boards on the decision making of their organisations. Pettigrew (1992) summarises many of these when he suggests that, in addition to superior expertise, information and advice available to management, there are norms of board conduct which restrict outsiders' abilities to act as strident independent voices; we shall return to this last point in greater detail below.

There are very few studies of the influence of governance in the recently proliferated partnership boards between health and local government. From a review of those published, Skelcher et al (2004) conclude: 'the theoretical connections between governance arrangements and organisational performance are poorly supported by empirical evidence' (p 14).

One of the most detailed studies in the field of health and local government is that of the role of the JCB in Somerset (see Peck et al, 2002a). Overall, the JCB spent much of its time receiving and/or approving papers prepared by a group of managers who were viewed as controlling the agenda and content of discussion. At the same time, the JCB set parameters on the content of these papers and could decline to approve papers that did not fit within them. Clearly, however, the JCB was not fulfilling the roles of setting policy and priorities in the way prescribed in government policy, and, indeed, in its own constitution. Freeman and Peck (2007), from a similar study in another English county, conclude that this JCB revealed itself as neither the engine room of corporate strategy nor as an interesting yet ineffectual diversion. Presumably these findings reflect the advocacy role of partnership leaders – the manipulation of the collaborative agenda – that is described by Armistead et al (2007; see Figure 2.2).

In addition to the problems identified by Pettigrew (1992), the summary by Cornforth (2003) of the various theories, interests, roles and models of governance is also important here (see Table 3.1). From this summary, he identifies three central tensions facing boards as a consequence of the differences in selection and contribution that might be consequent on these six different conceptions of governance:

- the tension between representative and professional boards;
- the tension between conformance and performance;
- the tension between controlling and partnering.

—

Table 3.1: Perspectives on organisational governance

Theory	Interests	Board members are	Board role	Model
Agency	Owners and managers have different interests	Owners' representatives	*Compliance/conformance* Safeguard owners' interests Oversee management Check compliance	Compliance
Stewardship	Owners and managers share interests	Experts	*Improve performance* Add value to top decisions/strategy Partner/support management	Partnership
Democratic perspective	Members/the public have different interests	Lay representatives	*Political* Represent constituents/members Reconcile conflicts Make policy Control executive	Democratic
Stakeholder	Stakeholders have different interests	Stakeholder representatives: elected or appointed by stakeholder groups	*Balancing stakeholder needs* Make policy strategy Control management	Stakeholder
Resource dependency	Stakeholders and organisations have different interests	Chosen for influence with key stakeholders	*Boundary spanning* Secure resources Maintain stakeholder relations Bringing an external perspective	Co-option
Managerial hegemony	Owners and managers have different interests	Owners' representatives	*Largely symbolic* Ratify decisions Give legitimacy Managers have real power	'Rubber stamp'

Source: After Cornforth (2003)

Of course, the most important point here is that boards may continually struggle with these tensions. For example, the democratic perspective of an elected local authority member on a partnership board concerning its governance task may stand in distinct contrast to the stakeholder perspective of an appointed member from the voluntary sector. Looked at another way, this may be one manifestation of the challenges that relate to *asymmetrical perceptions of legitimacy* contained in Figure 2.1 to which we return in Chapter 4. Furthermore, it may be within such governance arrangements that the three parallel fields of leadership identified by the ODPM (2005a) in the LSP study interact.

What can good governance do?

Although most of the Somerset JCB members recognised the limitations on its role, the majority did not therefore conclude that it was not worthwhile. In particular, the JCB seemed to participants to make at least three important symbolic contributions to the local health and social care system:

- Firstly, it was a symbol of interagency partnership between health and social services that set the context for partnership elsewhere in the local system.
- Secondly, it was a vehicle for sustaining the commitment to mental health of senior players within the NHS and the local authority.
- Thirdly, it was a way of bringing added public accountability to the commissioning and providing of healthcare.

This opens up the potential for a new avenue of thinking about governance, one that sees its importance as much in symbolic as instrumental terms.

The familiar view is that the work of boards is *instrumental*. On this view, they are there to make decisions, to engage in deliberation, to conciliate about content in conflicts. This is the view reflected in much of the prescriptive guidance on the role of boards. They are to be measured, on this account, by how far they decide efficiently and effectively on that on which they are officially supposed to decide

(Simon, 1997 [1945]). This is the view about boards commonly held by the public, and, apparently, by many policy makers.

The other view is that boards are for doing something organisationally important but which is unspoken (that is, does not appear on the agenda), and yet which gets done, successfully or otherwise, in the course of members being in the same place and speaking or remaining silent according to certain conventions. Boards are places where participants tell narratives about who they collectively are, sustain culture, organise shared emotions, sustain loyalty and conciliate over social relations in conflicts. This second view is that the work of boards is *symbolic* (Huff, 1988; Schwartzman, 1989; Weick, 1995). To connect with the earlier argument of Pettigrew (1992), these are the norms that discourage strident voices.

This starts to tell us what good governance can do. Good governance – as in the case of the Somerset JCB – is exhibited when boards undertake effectively the limited instrumental tasks available to them and do so in a manner that symbolises the collective and consensual approach to the delivery of public services in which they are involved. In the provision of public services by networks of organisations, good governance has to both *deliver legitimacy* (by engaging the appropriate range of stakeholders) and *perform legitimacy* (by building cohesion and commitment). Of course, poor governance may do neither. In support of this argument, Skelcher et al (2004) conclude, 'it is easier to establish the implications of governance arrangements for democratic performance than for organisational performance' (p 14); that is, it is easier to show that a specific form of governance has contributed to the symbolic performance (such as being seen to be legitimate) than it has to instrumental performance (such as actually achieving targets).

We think that this emerging theme provides three important messages for discussions of governance at a local level:

- Be clear when you are discussing governance with organisational partners that you are all talking about the same thing (perhaps using the Cornforth, 2003, framework).
- Be realistic about the limits of the instrumental impact of your governance arrangements.

- Be aware of the potential – both positive but also negative – of the symbolic impact of these arrangements.

We also believe that it helps to make the realities of governance more comprehensible, if perhaps no less complex.

Leadership as sense making and performance

Grint's recent accounts of leadership (for example, 2005a) have focused on the role of the leader in shaping the meaning that is given to situations by others; that is, he sees a significant part of leadership as consisting of influencing the sense making of others. In so doing, he is building on a growing trend in leadership theory – indeed organisational theory more generally – that is rooted in ideas originating in social constructionism (Berger and Luckmann, 1966). In this section we will present a short introduction to social constructionism and sense making.

Earlier, Grint (2000) observed that:

> Leadership is the world of the performing arts, the theatre of rhetorical skill, of negotiating skills, and of inducing the audience to believe in the world you paint with words and props. (p 28)

In so doing, he is describing the leadership role in sense making as a form of performance. This section will also, therefore, explore the sorts of performances that leaders might give in order to shape the views of others. In both cases, it is worth being clear from the outset that our view of the role of the leader in partnerships is, in the terms used by Bardach (1998), more about advocacy (or, in our words, 'manipulation') than it is about facilitation (where we doubt that a 'neutral' position for a leader is possible even if it was desirable).

Social constructionism and sense making

Social constructionism (see Burr, 1995) asserts that:

- our knowledge of the world is partial and very specific to the historic and cultural circumstances in which it is created or shared;
- this knowledge is co-constructed through interactions between people;
- knowledge (and the consequent social action) changes over time to produce numerous possible social constructions.

The theory suggests that the meanings that we attribute to our experience (be they social problems or network objectives) are thus:

- *multiple*, because each of us has our own;
- *negotiated*, because we seek to find common ground with others;
- *contested*, because finding such common ground can be difficult;
- *transient*, because we are frequently discovering new meanings in these conversations and discarding old ones.

Social constructionism, therefore, suggests that our human interactions have the power to shape the attitudes and behaviours of other members of organisations. In organisational theory, the particular term that has come to represent this phenomenon is 'sense making' (for example, Weick, 1995), which we introduced briefly in Chapter 1. Box 3.1 summarises the seven distinguishing features of sense making that Weick describes.

The importance of Weick's work to leadership is that it emphasises the potential for interventions by leaders to change the way in which organisational pasts, presents and futures are interpreted (for an example, see Pye, 1995). Beyond the organisation, social constructionism and sense making also suggest that policy problems, for example, those 'wicked' issues that need to be addressed by partnerships, do not arrive ready-made, but rather, have to be described, defined and named in a process that is typically called framing (Goffman, 1974). The way in which problems are framed – either nationally or locally – will also restrict the range of responses considered realistic.

Box 3.1: Weick's seven properties of sense making

1. It is grounded in the importance of sense making in the construction of the identity of the self (and of the organisation): 'who I am as indicated by discovery of how and what I think'.

2. It is retrospective in its focus on sense making as rendering meaningful lived experience: 'to learn what I think, I look back over what I said earlier'.

3. It recognises that people produce at least part of the environment (for example, the constraints and opportunities) within which they are sense making: 'I create the object to be seen and inspected when I say or do something'.

4. It stresses that sense making is a social process undertaken with others: 'what I say and single out and conclude are determined by who socialised me and how I was socialised, as well as by the audience I anticipate will audit the conclusions I reach'.

5. It argues that sense making is always ongoing in that it never starts and it never stops (even though events may be chopped out of this flow in order to be presented to others): 'my talking is spread across time, competes for attention with other ongoing projects, and is reflected on after it is finished, which means my interests may already have changed'.

6. It acknowledges that sense making is typically based on cues, where one simple and familiar item can initiate a process that encompasses a much broader range of meanings and implications: 'the "what" that I single out and embellish as the content of the thought is only a small proportion of the utterance that becomes salient because of context and personal dispositions'.

7. It is driven by plausibility rather than accuracy: 'I need to know enough about what I think to get on with my projects but no more, which means that sufficiency and plausibility take precedence over accuracy'.

Source: Derived from Weick (1995, pp 61-2), in Hardacre and Peck (2005)

—

In what ways is leadership a performance?

Let us return first to Weick's fourth property of sense making as a social process. The use of the word 'audience', both here and in the earlier quotation by Grint (2000), suggest that one aspect of leadership is that of the performer telling a story that is being tailored to be plausible (another term used by Weick) to this 'audience'. In most accounts of leadership, attention is paid to the performer (leader) at the expense of the stories that they tell or the audiences (potential followers) that they address. In the next few paragraphs, we will outline the practical benefits of focusing more on the stories and audiences in a context where we have already established – in Chapter 2 – that the most important apparent attribute of leaders in networks is *relational competence*. We will argue that the attribution of *relational competence* (or, for that matter, *integrity* or *commitment*) to a partnership leader is a consequence of the positive response of a range of audiences to the stories that they hear and read:

> Certain events are performances and other events less so. There are limits to what "is" a performance. But just about anything can be studied "as" performance. Something "is" a performance when historical and social context, convention, usage, and tradition say it is ... from the vantage of cultural practice, some actions will be deemed performances and others not; and this will vary from culture to culture, historical period to historical period. (Schechner, 2003, p 38)

The origins of performance as an academic discipline lie in accounts of ritual within anthropology, specifically the rites and ceremonies that enact social relationships (Bell, 1997). One of the key ideas in this literature is that of *restored behaviour*, defined as the 'physical, verbal or virtual actions that are not-for-the-first-time; that are prepared or rehearsed' (Schechner, 2003, p 29). Broadly speaking, in this tradition the emphasis is on deliberate performance; that is, on occasions where the event 'is' a performance, for examples, religious ceremonies or JCB meetings (this is a key point as we are talking about performing not acting – think Rowan Williams, Archbishop of Canterbury, not Rowan Atkinson in 'Blackadder'). We have discussed in the previous section the importance of the symbolic aspects of governance and we expand briefly on this here.

Effective ritual performance relies on the shared understandings of performer, co-participants and audience about the rules and purposes of the performance being given. Drawing on the insights of Goffman (1959), a four-stage approach can be applied to boards as rituals (see Table 3.2 for examples). Freeman and Peck (2007) use this approach in their analysis of a public board that, at least in its early days, struggled to be an effective ritual. They identify that there were problems with each of the four stages (Table 3.2). As a consequence of these problems, the board took to having private pre-meetings (quite literally, rehearsals). The relevance to leading in partnerships is that if such rituals both serve to endorse the framing given to problems and to enact social relationships (see Peck et al, 2004b) then leaders need to give careful consideration to the creation and maintenance of these fora. Indeed, many boards already acknowledge the benefits of innovations in setting and staging by organising, for example, member seminars within the timetable of board meetings. Nonetheless, given that such boards are also the place

Table 3.2: Four-stage approach of performance

Stages	Description	Practical example (from Freeman and Peck, 2007)
Scripting	The selection of the participants	Only PCT non-executives were selected to be members along with county councillors
Settings	The physical environment in which the interactions between these actors take place including the props that are available in those settings	The board table was laid out with nameplates as for a typical council meeting with PCT members down one side and county councillors down the other
Staging	The deliberate attempts to manipulate these interactions (for example, by the way in which papers are introduced and presented)	One draft strategy was unceremoniously rejected by the board because it did not conform to expectations about format
Performance	The manner in which the interaction takes place in the moment	The adversarial rather than consensual atmosphere in which discussions took place

where *asymmetrical power relations* and *perceptions of legitimacy* may be played out (as is the case in case study reported by Freeman and Peck, 2007), then once again it seems it is the setting within which leadership in partnership takes place that gives the role its distinctiveness.

At the same time, Schechner (2003) argues that '[M]any events and behaviours are one time events. Their "oneness" is a function of context, reception, and the countless ways bits of behavior can be organized, performed, and displayed' (p 29). If much of the work of boundary spanners takes place in more informal settings, and attributions of *integrity* and *commitment* are essential to their positive impact, then this will call for one-off performances in tailoring a broadly consistent narrative that remains relevant to the interests of a range of audiences. This will call for significant discipline on the part of the leader. The great opportunity of performances by leaders that shape sense making by an audience is that everything that s/he says or writes will have an impact. At the same time, the great burden of performances by leaders that shape sense making by an audience is that everything that s/he says or writes will have an impact!

We think that there are three important overall messages that arise from this discussion (outlined in Box 3.2).

Box 3.2: Key messages about partnership leaders and sense making

- The role of leaders in shaping the meaning that partners attach to the network – in particular in the framing of the problems to be addressed and their potential solutions – may be crucial.
- In intervening in sense making, leaders need to give as much careful attention to their narrative and their audience as they may already do to their own performance.
- The consideration of formal meetings as rituals reveals some practical issues that leaders need to bear in mind in their design and delivery, especially as such events are central to creating and maintaining social relations between partners.

Leadership and place making

As suggested earlier, the nature of public sector commissioning is altering fundamentally, taking on a different role to that traditionally assumed. Much of the research which has explored relationships between health and local authority partners has typically concentrated on specific areas such as joint commissioning, integrated provision, pooled budgets and joint appointments, rather than on the overall relationship between PCTs and local government. Yet arguably at this point, more than ever, health and social care are so important to each other that there is an opportunity to fundamentally re-think their relationship (Glasby et al, 2006). As Glasby and his colleagues suggest, increasingly PCTs will be required to move beyond traditional notions of corporate governance and become embedded in and fundamental to their local communities. As Wade et al (2006) argue, PCTs must fulfil a 'voice' function and reflect the views and demands of local people within their commissioning decisions. Accusations of a 'democratic deficit' have long been made against the NHS (Cooper et al, 1995; Klein and New, 1998; Hunter, 1999), whereas due to their accountability structures local authorities are thought to carry more of a local mandate (see Chapter 4 for more on this topic).

Central to the Lyons Review of local government (Lyons Inquiry, 2006) is the notion that local authorities should act as 'place shapers'. Local authorities should build and shape local identity, represent the community, regulate harmful and disruptive behaviours, maintain cohesiveness of the community, help to resolve disagreements, work to make the local economy more successful, understand and meet local needs and work with others on complex challenges (Lyons Inquiry, 2006, p 8). Arguably, health is so important to people's concept of place and identity that local authorities must work with PCTs in order to be able to deliver on this 'place-shaping' agenda (Glasby et al, 2006). Lyons expands on this theme, suggesting:

> Fundamentally, I see place-shaping as a way of describing my view that the ultimate purpose of local government should not be solely to manage a collection of public services that

> take place within an area, but rather to take responsibility for
> the well-being of an area and the people who live there, and
> to promote their interests and their future. (Lyons Inquiry,
> 2006, p 39)

In order for health and social care services to be able to deliver on
the difficult agendas laid out for them, and to confront a number of
the cross-cutting challenges that they currently face, they will need to
increasingly work together – and with other key local stakeholders – to
engage the population and produce a vision of their local 'place'. Only
by involving local stakeholders in such a process will public services
be able to deliver services which people want and need, and which
the public will be willing to pay for and engage with.

Cresswell (1996) suggests that there is an interaction between the
subjective and objective, between ideas and practices and between
cultural and economic geography rippled through the concept of
place which itself is both material and abstract. In other words, place
is more than simply a portion of geographic space, but is materially
and imaginatively constructed by many different types of people. It
is important to note that place building and sense making do not
just invoke cultural and social aspects, but also material artefacts. This
is also supported by actor network theory which suggests a leader
is 'a person who has learned to see connections and relationships
between people and things and develop the networks of knowledge,
information, space, and social capital necessary for managing and
increasing organisational or system performance. In essence ... leaders
have learned to develop a level of personal influence that helps them
serve as attractors – important nodes of connectors – in a vast array
of potential networks in a system' (Sidle and Warzynski, 2003, p 42).
As such, there is an opportunity for local leaders to become involved
in working with local populations to make sense of the locality and
the issues which it faces and to shape the ways in which its pasts,
presents and futures are conceived. Leaders will no longer simply be
able to defend individual institutions, but must demonstrate how it is
that agencies collectively feed into and contribute to local public life.

Clearly the issues of social constructionism and sense making may be useful resources to draw on within these processes.

Although a growing number of philosophers, ethnographers and geographers have been interested in the processes by which place comes into being through a practical process of place making (Rodman, 1992), there is relatively little research which explicitly considers leadership and place making. In a study of the failure of a proposed computer-driven public transportation system in Paris, Latour (1996) suggests that the top-down approach which the leadership adopted failed, firstly, to build adequate support for the change by taking into account the interests and needs of the different stakeholders and failed, secondly, to resolve disputes with those who opposed the policies. He concludes that successful place making requires strategic alliances formed on compromise between stakeholder leaders that can rally networks of interest in a shared perception of a deliverable socially constructed reality. There are clearly elements of the transformational model of leadership suggested here, but the situation is more nuanced than this one case study alone demonstrates.

However important, the level of the tasks facing leaders seeking to engage in the place-shaping agenda cannot be underestimated. As previously suggested, the process of leadership in place making will likely need to span the three parallel fields of leadership suggested in the LSP evaluation (ODPM, 2005a; see Box 2.3) – political leadership, leadership from partner organisations and leadership within the community. Yet these parallel fields may hold different beliefs in terms of what they value in terms of leadership styles (that is, what sorts of performances may attract the attribution of 'good leadership'). As the LSP national evaluation demonstrates, political leadership roles have tended to be under-estimated and under-examined. Politicians in positions of authority must build consensus and contribute to political legitimacy, but also engage backbench councillors, community leaders and other key interests. In this respect, there may be a range of key lessons that partnership leaders may learn from political leaders, particularly given that Alimo-Metcalfe's work on transformational leadership (for example, Alimo-Metcalfe and Alban-Metcalfe, 2003) has demonstrated that NHS leaders do not emphasise the importance of political acumen in their assessment of effective leaders. As Storey (2004a) suggests, political leaders require three 'meta-capabilities': big picture sense making; interorganisational representation; and an ability to deliver change (Figure 3.1). This suggests that while political leaders are imbued with executive agency functions, and that these are necessary to deliver on certain aspects of their roles, political leaders also need to be able to be inclusive and set out a wider vision which is, to some degree, acceptable to all.

Figure 3.1: Competencies of political leaders

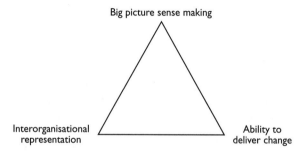

Big picture sense making

Interorganisational representation

Ability to deliver change

Source: Adapted from Storey (2004a)

Not only will place-shaping leadership processes be required to span these three parallel fields, but they will also be required to do so during the different time spans of the life of any partnerships (as previously outlined). As such, place-shaping leaders will encounter a number of the challenges set out in Figure 2.1 at different points and be required to use appropriate leadership attributes in order to deal with or overcome these difficulties.

The three key messages from this section are:

• Particular partnerships may need, in the near future, to be embedded in a much closer set of organisational relationships between public agencies in a locality where they become central and not to some extent marginal to the organisations concerned.

- 'Civic' leaders will have to be accustomed to working with numerous stakeholders with a variety of points of view derived from divergent forms of legitimacy.
- In these circumstances, the ability of leaders to sense make with and on behalf of these stakeholders will be crucial to their impact.

Having so far problematised the nature of leadership and management in interagency settings and outlined a number of the hot topics relating to this area, the following chapter aims to set out a number of useful frameworks and concepts which leaders and managers may employ in practice in order to produce more effective interagency relationships.

Reflective exercises

1. What do you understand by the term 'governance'? Compare and contrast your perspectives with those of a colleague from a different professional or organisational background.

2. Think about the formal governance structures of a partnership you have read about or have experience of. What did these consist of and what did they do in practice? (You may want to draw on Table 3.1 here.) To what degree is the influence of these structures instrumental and to what degree is it symbolic?

3. Think about someone who you consider to be a successful leader. In what ways might their actions be considered performances? How does this leader draw on sense-making processes (for example, what sort of stories does s/he tell)?

4. Why do you think that health and social care leaders might wish to engage with place-shaping processes? What challenges might this entail? Which leadership attributes will be most appropriate to these processes?

Further reading and resources

For detailed studies of formal governance structures and their impacts on organisational performance see Peck et al's (2002a, 2004b), Glasby and Peck's (2004) and Freeman and Peck's (2007) accounts.

For the Audit Commissions critique of the accountability of partnerships see the 2005 paper *Governing partnerships.*

For an introduction to social constructivism see Berger and Luckman's (1966) *The social construction of reality.* See Grint's (2005a, 2005b) accounts which link leadership in with concepts of social constructivism.

Weick's (1995) *Sensemaking in organizations* is a seminal account of issues surrounding sense making and is a useful introduction to this area.

See Goffman (for example, 1974) for further information on framing and the stages of performance.

A useful paper which sets out the importance of place making to health and social care organisations is Glasby et al's (2006) *Creating 'NHS Local'.*

4

Useful frameworks
and concepts

Let us now turn to the specific challenges that partnerships face and that were summarised in Figure 2.1. We will focus in particular on those that may be amenable to local leaders (as opposed to ones that arise from national policy, legal requirements and so on). In the course of this chapter, we will look at a broad range of writing and research, reaching beyond material arising from specific discussions of partnership and leadership (although some of the responses to these challenges have hopefully already been suggested in the review of the literature in the previous chapters). In so doing, we are following the argument of McCray and Ward (2003) who maintain that, without either a clear understanding of the tensions of policy – and its implementation at local level – or a detailed analysis of professional roles in the light of political or economic factors, it is difficult to deal with the barriers to change that will arise. In these circumstances, it seems crucial that the partnership leader has the widest understanding possible of the context in which s/he is operating. The next five sections again assume that, in practice, many (if not most) such leaders will be, in the terms explored in Chapter 2, 'active advocates' rather than 'neutral facilitators'. Finally, however, it is important to stress that what follows can only briefly introduce some of the most helpful concepts and readers may want to pursue further those ideas that resonate with them.

Lack of a shared framework

Lack of a shared framework (of authority, accountability and procedures) between collaborators has long been identified as a source of significant challenge (and, in fewer cases, of strength where difference is seen as diversity or maybe, in the language of the framework explored later in this chapter, 'requisite variety'). This disparity is often raised in relation to the budget cycle and the use of financial resources (not surprisingly given that *resource exchange* is such a common form of network). In these circumstances, where many of the rules are outside of local discretion, the best approach that a leader can adopt may be to understand the nature of the difference and the problems and paradoxes that might ensue. There is some evidence in the literature that effective partnerships shape the organisational arrangements of the partners. This clearly takes time (and has been called 'negotiated order' by Emery and Trist, 1973). Nevertheless, it is perhaps partially frustration with the problems that arise consequent to these issues of authority, accountability and procedures within networks that prompt policy makers to suggest solutions that move collaborations towards more hierarchical organisational forms (for example, care trusts). Yet such approaches may merely serve to delay the impact or to move the location of these problems (as Hudson, 2004, has repeatedly pointed out in relation to care trusts).

Expectations, however, are more open to influence. It is worth, at this point, recalling the leadership model of Grint (2005a) that we introduced in Chapter 1. He argues that the consensus – such as there is – about a model of leadership is based on

> ... a naïve assumption because it underestimates the extent to which the context or situation is actively constructed by the leader, leaders, and/or decision makers. In effect, leadership involves the social construction of the context that both legitimates a particular form of action and constitutes the world in the process. If that rendering of the context is successful – for there are usually contending and competing renditions – the newly constituted context then limits the alternatives available such that those involved begin to act differently. (Grint, 2005a, pp 1470-1)

(We have said more about social construction in our discussion of sense making in Chapter 3.) Further, Grint argues that 'where no one can be certain about what needs to be done to resolve a Wicked Problem then the more likely decision-makers are to seek a collective response' (p 1478). This suggests that expectations – that is, the nature of the 'wicked' problem to be solved by a partnership – can be shaped at a local level, albeit that the parameters of these expectations will be more or less constrained by national policy and local factors. The framing of the problem is crucial, for in the framing of the problem lies the potential for some solutions to be privileged and others marginalised.

There are two other ways of thinking about this topic that are illuminating: complexity theory and 'big windows and little windows'. We shall briefly look at each here.

Complexity theory has become one of the most fashionable ideas within organisational theory in recent times (for an overview, see Sweeney, 2005). One of the most influential writers, Stacey (for example, 1999), has conceptualised the agreement/uncertainty matrix (see Figure 4.1). Within this matrix, the vertical axis represents, for our purposes, *agreement* between partners about the nature of the issues that the partnership is going to address. *Certainty*, represented by the horizontal axis, suggests how sure partners are about the cause and effect linkages, that is, assuming we are at 'A', doing 'B' will lead to 'C'. Where a partnership leader is operating close to the bottom left-hand

Figure 4.1: The Stacey (1999) matrix developed by Zimmerman et al (1998)

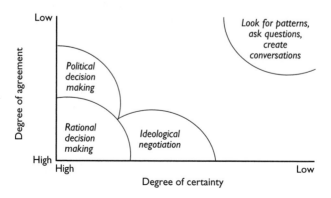

corner – where agreement and certainty between partners are high – they can usually draw on prior experience to inform action (this is the tame problem of Grint's matrix in Figure 1.3 which he argues requires management, not leadership).

However, most partnerships deal with 'wicked' problems, where either agreement or certainty – or both – are absent. In Figure 4.1, Zimmerman et al (1998) have developed Stacey's original matrix to explore further the response to these wicked problems. Where there is considerable certainty, for example, about which outcomes are desirable, but much less agreement about how these can be delivered, they argue leaders are in the realm of political decision making. In contrast, where there is high certainty that we are at 'A' and that doing 'B' will lead to 'C', but no agreement that 'C' is a preferred destination, then they suggest that leaders are in the domain of ideological negotiation.

In the absence of both agreement and certainty, Sweeney suggests that leaders are in the realm of complexity and follows the advice of Margaret Wheatley (2001) in recommending that they build networks, enhance communication, work collectively and allow direction to emerge. Henry Mintzberg (for example, Mintzberg and van der Heyden, 1999) contends that we should look for patterns in participants' responses (and there are links forward to the discussion of culture here). Ralph Stacey (for example 1999) argues that, in these circumstances, leaders should design opportunities for conversations (for example, stakeholder conferences, open space events) that facilitate new forms of consensus to emerge. These fora are presumably the settings within which leaders can pose the questions that Grint (2005a) maintains can shape the framing of the problem and the contours of the solution.

Another perspective on what leaders might do outside of the zone of rational decision making – perhaps in the course of the conversations aimed at creating consensus – is to adopt Exworthy and Powell's (2004) 'big windows and little windows' approach. Previous work on national policy by Kingdon (1995) suggested that an issue gets on the policy agenda when it brings together three 'streams':

- the *problem stream* which outlines the nature of the challenge(s) to be resolved;

—

- the *policy stream* which comprises the proposals to tackle the challenge;
- the *politics stream* which consists of the interests of stakeholders.

The 'big windows' open – and policy is made – when these three elements are aligned within national government. Exworthy and Powell (2004) suggest that policy that requires interagency collaboration is best implemented when these three streams are also aligned at a local level (thus, the 'little windows'; see Figure 4.2). This suggests that partnership leaders attempting to gain commitment to action around a wicked issue need to use these conversations to frame the problem in such a way that it connects with the political predilections of the agencies involved and comes complete with a policy solution that offers the prospect of progress and/or resolution.

Figure 4.2: Congruence of big and little windows: vertical and horizontal dimensions

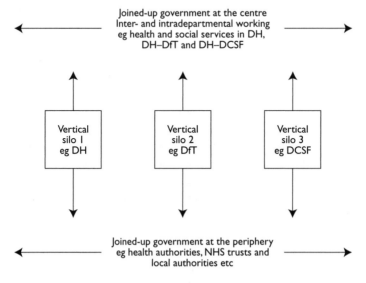

Joined-up government at the centre
Inter- and intradepartmental working
eg health and social services in DH,
DH–DfT and DH–DCSF

Vertical silo 1 eg DH

Vertical silo 2 eg DfT

Vertical silo 3 eg DCSF

Joined-up government at the periphery
eg health authorities, NHS trusts and
local authorities etc

Notes: DH = Department of Health; DfT = Department for Transport; DCSF = Department for Children, Schools and Families.
Source: Adapted from Exworthy and Powell (2004, p 269)

Incompatible cultures and values

There has been much written about broader aspects of culture in health and social partnerships (much of it by the current authors; see Peck et al, 2001; Peck and Crawford, 2004; Peck and Dickinson, 2008: forthcoming). This is because in discussions of partnership working between health and social care one issue seems to recur more than any other: culture. Furthermore, it appears simultaneously to be both an aspiration for partnerships (for example, to change culture) and an obstacle to partnerships (for example, conflicts rooted in culture). The literature suggests that this latter perspective is well founded. Organisations may have such fundamentally different ways of framing issues, reacting to problems and interpreting procedural rules that bringing such different cultures together will lead to a situation of 'us versus them' (Marks and Mirvis, 1992). The aim of this section is to summarise some of the key issues relating to partnership working, drawing on Peck and Dickinson (2008: forthcoming).

Most accounts of culture assume what Meyerson and Martin (1987) call an *integration model*. This sees culture as something that organisations possess and which is therefore broadly recognisable and consistent across them. On this view, culture is an influence that can promote integration within organisations (thus two divergent cultures may need to be reconciled when organisations work in partnership) and may be manipulated in relatively predictable ways in order to enhance integration.

A second approach identified by Meyerson and Martin (1987) conceptualises culture as more pluralistic, with disparate cultures being held by different interest groups within the same organisation. On this view, culture is an influence which may once again inhibit integration (and thus partnership), but where the various cultures may be open to manipulation, in particular in relation to the ways in which they interact. This is the *difference model* of culture.

The third perspective discussed by Meyerson and Martin (1987) – the *ambiguity model* – considers it to be more local and personal than the other two, constantly being negotiated and re-negotiated between individuals and groups within the organisation. These patterns of creation and re-creation of culture may be influenced by the organisation within which and the interest groups between which they take place, but it is the one that perhaps offers the least prospect of predictable manipulation.

In their study of partnership development in Somerset, Peck et al (2001) identified the presence of all three of these levels of culture. Broadly, discussions with managers revealed an assumption of an integration model of culture, those with professional groups focused on professional difference (see below) and those with staff in localities suggested considerable negotiation and re-negotiation of culture consistent with the ambiguity model. In another account, Wistow and Waddington (2006) identify the *difference* model of culture in practice, while the collaborating agencies continued with the assumption that pursuit of an *integration* model would create an effective partnership; the authors report how the partnership process ran into difficulties due to 'basic incompatibilities, largely derived from the mismatch in cultures' (p 14). Wistow and Waddington summarise the characteristics of the NHS and social services partners (illustrated in Table 4.1). These are not uncommon characterisations of health and social care and relate in part to the differing professional 'models' of care which are frequently typified as underpinning health and social care (again, we shall return to this in a later section). Clearly, therefore, deploying the Meyerson and Martin framework has potential for aiding both interpretation of and intervention in culture.

Table 4.1: Differences in characterisation of the NHS and social services partners

NHS	Social services
Treatment	Care
National targets	Local needs
Must-dos	Local discretion
Universal services	Focus on vulnerable
Procedurally regimented and very top-down in style	Practical focus but has difficulty with strategy and planning

Source: Based on Wistow and Waddington (2006, p 14)

—

Is the management of culture possible? It appears that the difference and ambiguity views of culture offer less hope to the would-be manipulators of culture than the integration model. Parker (2000) offers two conclusions from his review of the culture literature (and his case studies based in healthcare settings): the first is that 'cultural management in the sense of creating an enduring set of shared beliefs is impossible' (p 228); on the other hand, he suggests that 'it seems perverse to argue that the "climate", "atmosphere", "personality", or culture of an organisation cannot be consciously altered' (p 229). This is broadly the view adopted by the authors, although we also acknowledge – along with Bate et al (2000) – the poor track record of corporate cultural change programmes that do not simultaneously look at the prospects for changes in authority, accountability and procedures.

Is structural change enough to change culture? It would appear that structural change – the predominant tool for cultural change in Somerset, for example – may not be enough; the creation of a partnership trust (and associated innovations such as the co-location of health and social care staff) was not in itself a sufficient condition to create the desired cultural changes during the first three years (albeit that might be an optimistic time frame within which to expect such changes). Indeed, in the short term at least, structural change may have served to strengthen attachment to existing professional cultures (see Peck et al, 2002b). With these caveats in mind, this section now briefly examines a range of tools for and approaches to interventions in culture in organisations.

In a systematic review of quantitative measures of organisational culture that have either been validated and used in healthcare settings or appeared to have potential for use in such settings, Scott et al (2003b) identify a total of 13 instruments (illustrated in Box 4.1). Scott and his co-authors (2003a) argue for the pragmatic selection of an instrument based on the purpose and context of any assessment. The researchers classify measurement tools as either typological (in which assessment results in one or more types of organisational culture) or a dimensional approach (which describes a culture by its position on

—

a number of continuous variables). They identify four things to think about in utilising these tools:

- *Levels*, that is, are you looking at the central core or more superficial manifestations?
- *Triangulation*, that is, are you drawing messages following comparisons of data from various sources?
- *Sampling*, that is, are you asking a representative number of staff?
- *Analysis*, for example, are you going to explore the results by professional group or by geographical locality?

Box 4.1: Quantitative organisational culture measures

Typological approaches
- Competing Values Questionnaire
- Harrison's Organisational Ideology Questionnaire
- Quality Improvement Implementation Survey

Dimensional approaches
- Organisational Culture Inventory
- Hospital Culture Questionnaire
- Nursing Unit Culture Assessment Tool
- Practice Culture Questionnaire
- MacKenzie's Culture Questionnaire
- Survey of Organisational Culture
- Corporate Culture Questionnaire
- Core Employee Opinion Questionnaire
- Hofstede's Organisational Culture Questionnaire
- Organisational Culture Survey

Source: After Scott et al (2003b)

The management literature contains many examples of claimed 'makeovers' of organisational culture (for example, Shirley, 2000; Bernick, 2001), and these may prove illuminating to those seeking to address organisational dysfunction apparently rooted in poor fits

—

between cultures. Nonetheless, Davies et al (2000) urge a cautious reassessment of the possibilities for cultural transformation in the NHS which would involve sensitivity to subcultural differences, honouring current achievements and consideration of the needs, fears and motivations of diverse staff groups.

These factors are echoed in those that the (extensive) literature on mergers suggest are crucial to the effective bringing together of organisations. Peck et al (2006) summarise these factors (Box 4.2).

Box 4.2: Crucial factors in the merger experience

- Create and communicate a vision that sets out the purpose of the transition.
- Adopt a participative and open style.
- Attend to sense making, helping people through the unpredictable elements of changes and preserving routine for them where possible.
- Managing human resources should be the main activity of senior managers, and not just something that human resources professionals do.
- Communicate the changes and latest developments relentlessly for people will be hungry for information.
- Set up clear transitional structures that incorporate senior people, and that are able to enact the transition promptly.
- Focus on the psychological and development needs of staff.
- Assess/audit the culture of each of the merging organisations and use this knowledge as part of a careful strategy for acknowledging the differences between organisations.
- Measure the impact of the transition for at least three years.

Finally, is there a clear link between organisational culture and organisational performance? From their exhaustive study in healthcare, Scott et al (2003b) decide that empirical studies do not provide clear answers, while noting that the available research is small in quantity, mixed in quality and variable in methodology (thus making comparisons between studies difficult). This is, of course, very different to the confident assertions of the authors of the 'culture cookbooks'. However, it seems counter to our intuition and our experience to deny any such link, challenging as this may be to prove to the satisfaction of researchers. Ultimately, consideration of both the literature and previous experience suggests that through reflecting on and intervening in organisational culture(s) with sense and sensitivity, partially through re-designing organisational structures when opportunities arise, managers and practitioners can achieve some change in that culture, while being aware that such interventions may well have unanticipated aspects.

Asymmetrical perceptions of legitimacy

Incompatible cultures and values are often manifested by agencies holding *asymmetrical perceptions of legitimacy*, typically arguing that their organisation has more legitimacy that their partners. These perceptions are frequently long-standing, both organisationally and personally. While they can be – and are – held between all partners (for example, statutory bodies can question how representative voluntary groups are of either their members or the broader client group), they are probably most common in the view of local authority-elected members of the non-executives in the NHS; it is usually framed as being about the latter possessing a 'democratic deficit'. A little history may be helpful here.

In a previous generation, policy makers in the 1970s attempted to foster a closer working relationship between the NHS and local government over the implementation of community care through so-called joint planning arrangements. The relationship between the appointed members of the NHS and the elected members of local government took place within joint consultative committees (JCCs). Wistow and Hardy (1991) conclude that, despite extensive efforts, there was widespread agreement among participants that this machinery was not successful. More recently, in the early 1990s, local authority nominees were summarily removed from the boards of NHS bodies as the then government sought to bring in more private sector expertise. Over the course of the past five years

—

there have been tensions between the NHS Confederation and the Local Government Association over, for instance, the proposal to create care trusts (see Glasby and Peck, 2003).

As an example of this, Sullivan and Skelcher (2002) summarise recent research into the 'democratic deficit' in regeneration partnerships, suggesting that many partnership boards are much less transparent and accountable than most committees in local authorities have traditionally been (see Table 4.2). They suggest this is because the latter have a much more explicit democratic mandate and are subject to a series of statutory responsibilities concerning openness and communication with the public.

Table 4.2: The 'democratic deficit' in partnerships

What proportion of partnerships...	Study 1 Robinson and Shaw (2000) (%)	Study 2 Hall and Nevin (1998) (%)
Publish a delivery plan	75	n/a
Publish newsletters	60	65
Publish paper for meetings[a]	54	47
Have a code of conduct[a]	46	41
Hold publicly accessible board meetings[a]	46	29
Publish an annual report[a]	43	41
Hold annual general meetings open to the public[a]	29	n/a
Have a register of members' interests[a]	21	12
Have a memorandum of association[a]	n/a	41
Publish accounts[a]	n/a	35
Have standing orders[a]	n/a	35

Note: [a] indicates a statutory requirement on the local authority.
Source: Based on Sullivan and Skelcher (2002, p 151)

Elected member nominees on partnership boards may well encourage partnership boards to be as open as possible in the ways suggested in Table 4.2; this should probably be welcomed. However, it is important that local authorities – and in particular their elected members – recognise the legitimacy of NHS institutions, albeit that this legitimacy is derived from a different source than their own (and this may be another opportunity for partnership leaders to influence the sense making of colleagues; for further discussion of this topic, see Glasby and Peck, 2006). In addition, the NHS now has access to new forms of community accountability – through so-called foundation organisations – that may require local authority members to review their traditional perceptions of this perceived deficit.

Asymmetrical power relations

There are at least two distinct ways of thinking about this topic at an organisational level (we shall return to issues of power and professionals in the next section). The first – and probably most familiar – relates to the exercise of power where it is conceived of a sort of resource (where one agency or individual can be said to have more power than another). Numerous commentators over the years have added to the list of potential sources of power. In a recent summary Clegg et al (2005) include: information; expertise; credibility; stature and prestige; uncertainty; access to top-level managers and the control of money, sanctions and rewards; and control over resources. To this list might also be added legal prerogatives (such as formal accountability for use of public money). Pfeffer (1992) argues that it is crucial that leaders study these sources carefully: 'since we cannot otherwise hope to gain individual success in organisations or the success of the organisations [or, presumably, partnerships] themselves' (p 8).

Also in this tradition is the discussion of the so-called three dimensions of power (Lukes, 1974). This suggests that power can be exercised in three ways:

- *Direct decision making:* 'A has power over B to the extent that he can get B to do something B would not otherwise do' (for example, through contractual requirements) (Dahl, 1957, pp 202-3).
- *Non-decision making:* A prevents the issues or questions which are in B's interests, but not in A's, from surfacing (for example, through excluding items from the remit of the partnership board) (Bachrach and Baratz, 1962).
- *Defining interests:* A may exercise power over B 'by influencing, shaping or determining his very wants' (for example, through framing a problem in a particular way) (Lukes, 1974, p 23).

Bringing these strands together, Mintzberg (1983) articulated an elaborate architecture of the ways in which power is exercised in and around organisations. Of course, use of these frameworks may help partnership leaders to understand – perhaps even in their advocacy role to exploit – some of the asymmetries of power evident in the collaboration; it does not, however, serve to dissolve them.

More recent contributions have focused more on power as a property of relations rather than as an abstract resource derived from a variety of sources (for example, Clegg, 1989). On this account, we should be more interested in how power is manifest in practice. Clegg argues that his predecessors have focused too much on agency and not enough on two other aspects of power: the social and systemic elements that form the context within which individual interactions take place. He argues that the social element consists of the rules of meaning and membership within which power is exercised and the system elements comprise the methods of control and discipline that agencies use to ensure effective production.

Like a number of organisational theorists (and we will return to a more famous example below), Clegg seems here to be drawing on ideas of neo-Durkheimian institutionalist (NDIT) theory that was briefly introduced in Chapter 1. As the name suggests, this account draws on the work of Émile Durkheim, as developed by anthropologist Mary Douglas (for example, 1982) and her school. In *Suicide*, Durkheim (1951 [1897]) argued that there are two central dimensions along which forms of social organisation vary:

- *Social regulation:* the extent to which social life is governed by role, rule and given social fact or, alternatively, by the outcome of voluntarily entered relations (what Clegg terms the rules of meaning and membership).
- *Social integration:* the extent to which individual people are held accountable to larger collectivities (what Clegg terms the methods of control and discipline).

Cross-tabulating these two dimensions yields a classification of the basic forms of social organisation (see Figure 4.3). The cross-tabulation defines the four basic types. We will summarise these four types here, drawing out a number of key characteristics, including styles of sense making (as a potentially central area for intervention by leaders; see Pye, 2005) for each basic form. Figure 4.4 suggests the nature of the rituals that might be predominant in these basic forms.

Strong social regulation, together with strong social integration, provide the defining features of *hierarchical* systems. In a hierarchical order each rank has its place, and is due the appropriate respect for its role that it serves in the functioning of the entire system. The structure of social ties is dense at the top of the system, and less so as one moves down the order. In hierarchical systems, sense making is done authoritatively and is highly institutionalised through the more or less formal authorisation of narratives and myths. The UK civil service could be seen as an example of hierarchy.

In contrast, weak social regulation and weak social integration are the defining characteristics of *individualism.* Individuals can act with relative freedom, and in such settings those who can exploit their own skill or luck, or who can exploit gaps in the social structure to act as brokers, will achieve greater status on the basis not of role but of achievement and control of resources. In such settings, there are sparse social ties thus exhibiting structural holes within which such brokers operate. In these settings, the individual broker has the opportunity to become the leading sense maker for those around her or him. Small management consultancy companies could be seen as exemplifications of individualism.

Figure 4.3: The basic forms of social organisation

This figure should be read in conjunction with Figure 1.2.

Isolate *Strong regulation, weak integration*	**Hierarchy** *Strong regulation, strong integration*
Style of organisation: heavily constrained individuals acting opportunistically, unable to sustain trust save perhaps with close kin	*Style of organisation:* centrally ordered community eg bureaucratic organisation
Basis of power: domination	*Basis of power:* asymmetric status, rule- and role-based authorisation
Strategy: coping or survival-oriented behaviour, individual withdrawal	*Strategy:* regulation, control through systems of status based on role
Authority: weak, if any, among dominated isolates, temporary celebrity; otherwise, temporary despotism among dominating isolates	*Authority:* status-based, paternalistic, but with rule-bound discretion (in Weberian terms, bureaucratic)
Individualism *Weak regulation, weak integration*	**Enclave** *Weak regulation, strong integration*
Style of organisation: instrumental, entrepreneurial individuals eg markets	*Style of organisation:* internally egalitarian, but sharply marked boundaries with others; held together by shared commitment to moral principle eg sects, cults, movements, clubs
Basis of power: personal control of resources	*Basis of power:* constant personal and collective reaffirmation commitment
Strategy: brokering, negotiating for control of resources	*Strategy:* intense mutual support within enclave, confrontation of those outside
Authority: power-based; authority derives from ability to define opportunities and bestow rewards; in Weberian terms, merchant adventurer	*Authority:* in Weberian terms, charismatic, based on personal demonstration of marginally greater commitment to shared principle

Source: Adapted from Peck and 6 (2006)

—

Figure 4.4: Ritual forms associated with each basic form of authority

Isolate	Hierarchy
Exemplars of ritual style: satirical stand-up comedy	*Exemplars of ritual style:* procession
Emotions elicited in ritual, when successful in its own institutional terms: irony, ridicule, stoic will to endure	*Emotions elicited in ritual, when successful in its own institutional terms:* respectful deference for status, amour-propre for own role, commitment, sense of security
Emotions elicited when less successful: bitterness, sense of arbitrariness, opacity and banality	*Emotions elicited when less successful:* demoralisation, confusion and bemusement at complexity of institutions, sense of banality

Individualism	Enclave
Exemplars of ritual style: trade fair, street market	*Exemplars of ritual style:* religious revivalist meeting, militant picketing strikers meeting
Emotions elicited in ritual, when successful in its own institutional terms: aspiration, excitement, controlled envy for competitive rivalry	*Emotions elicited in ritual, when successful in its own institutional terms:* passionate commitment, collective effervescence, passionate rejection of outsiders and those seen as insiders who have betrayed the institution
Emotions elicited when less successful: insecurity, dejection at own defeat, frustration at what seems futile and self-defeating rivalry	*Emotions elicited when less successful:* schism

Source: Peck and 6 (2006)

Strong social integration and weak social regulation is the *enclave*, the club, the clan or the sect. Here, the voluntarily entered collective is held together only as long as shared commitment to some principle can sustain the complex systems of rules required to stave off schism. The boundaries of the voluntarily entered and sustained collectivity have to be defined fairly rigidly around membership of some kind, or else the enclave will quickly disintegrate. Sense making in such contexts is, as we should expect, a collective process, and has to cleave closely to the claims of principle around which the enclave is organised. User groups in mental health services could be characterised as enclaves.

Strong social regulation and weak social integration is the condition of the *isolate*. The isolate, being weakly bonded to others, lacks capabilities for collective action that all the other forms, even individualistically brokered systems, possess. Sense making in such conditions is peculiarly strained and attenuated. Self-employed and single-handed GPs in the UK NHS might be perceived as isolates.

Each one of these four basic institutional forms will possess its own patterns of authority, accountability and procedure and elicit a distinct worldview from its members (Feyerabend, 2000). The strong claim of NDIT is that institutions sustain themselves precisely to the extent that they can secure people to think in institutionally prescribed ways; only thereby will sufficient commitment be elicited from people to organise in the ways that the institution's principles call for. Conversely, institutions define the bounds of the unthinkable, that which is too threatening to the system on which the institution is organised to be permitted to be taken seriously. Each of these forms – and the hybrid forms that derive from them – therefore produces a style of sense making. Sense making is thus a profoundly social activity for it can only be done through social institutions (see Weick, 1995).

In creating partnerships, therefore, leaders are typically bringing together agencies with distinct ways of organising. This is the second – and less familiar – perspective for thinking about asymmetrical power relations; that is, the approach to authority, accountability and procedures – how power is conceptualised, legitimised and manifested – may differ significantly between partners.

There are two more important points to be made about this theoretical framework. Firstly, it is not a static classification but contains an account of how positive and negative feedback can change the balance between these ways of organising in given situations (again, see Peck and 6, 2006 and also 6 et al, 2006). Secondly, it recognises that most institutions will be hybrids of these basic forms, acting as sites where these feedback mechanisms will operate but also acknowledging that sustainable organisations may combine elements of all these four basic forms in their organisational settlements (what is often termed the principle of 'requisite variety').

This latter point is important for leaders of partnerships. It suggests that in creating and maintaining collaborations between agencies, they should be aware of both the inevitability, but also the desirability of allowing each way of organising to be incorporated. Over-assertion of a specific way of organising favoured by one partner may quickly serve to alienate others and lead to conflict and/or resistance (for a worked example of this in relation to a JCB see Peck et al, 2004b; Peck and 6, 2006; the main conclusions are summarised in Box 4.3 below).

In conclusion, therefore, it seems that both perspectives on asymmetries of power are illuminating. The first highlights the manner in which power – seen as a resource – may be held both in varying degrees and from different sources among partners. The second provides an account of the contrasting ways of organising between partners and how power may thus be differentially legitimised and exercised in each. This also focuses attention on the social and systemic boundaries within which any exercise of power by individuals will be shaped and constrained. Perhaps the key message for leaders of partnership is that of the importance of requisite variety; the most sustainable networks may be those that allow each way of organising to be influential on the patterns of authority, accountability and procedure that are adopted.

Box 4.3: The Somerset JCB

The Somerset JCB was initially a hierarchical ritual order that at first allowed some contained space for GP isolates. The preferred rhetorical style of the latter within the meetings was a form of ridicule, questioning the motives and competencies of managers. At first, the hierarchical order attempted to accommodate these isolate contributions by referring presented and challenged papers back for further work rather than the JCB accepting them. In time, the hierarchy removed the threat by replacing the GPs with the chief executives from primary care organisations who were familiar with the meeting-as-procession. The isolate form was also represented on the JCB by the single elected member drawn from the minority party on the county council. At the meetings, he became, interestingly, in terms of Figure 4.3, the sit-down comedian, making ironic comments on the business of the JCB.

Subsequently confronted by user and carer representatives, the ritual order was again under pressure. Determined to avoid allowing the JCB to become a space for enclave organisation – and alarmed by the possibility that the 'personal' matters raised by users and carers would create a space for collective effervescence among them – the proposal to create a separate meeting with a distinct ritual order was a predictable hierarchical response.

The JCB, therefore, went through two successive hybrid forms. The first was a hierarchical isolate form and the second was a hierarchical enclave form. Neither hybrid was an entirely happy or stable affair. Its instability showed up in the difficulty the JCB found in stabilising its ritual order and, therefore, in entirely binding all participants in to the structure. Neither the GPs nor the user and carer representatives settled wholly or easily into the norms or the rhetoric, and the ritual did not elicit in them the emotions required for a successful performance in hierarchical terms.

Source: Edited from Peck and 6 (2006)

—

Different professional discourses

One of the most frequently referred to difficulties in terms of health and social care partnerships are the different professional discourses that exist in these organisations and which might serve 'tribal interests' (Hunter, 1996); there is a clear link here to the notion of enclaves discussed in the previous section. Individuals are selectively recruited and socialised into professional groups that are essentially self-interested. Such groups will aim to protect themselves against others; often professional identity constitutes a valued part of an individual's personal identity (Evetts, 1999). This process of socialisation encompasses place, education, training and everyday experiences. In terms of education, professionals are not simply educated in terms of formal skills, but also less tangible 'informal' skills. This might include exposing individuals to the particular values, cultures, language and norms that tend to be associated with that profession. Via these processes individuals become part of a particular professional discourse providing a social boundary that defines what can be said about a specific topic. They become institutionalised into particular ways of sense making (and thus behaving) (for examples of the divergent stories of their theory and practice told by professional groups working in mental health teams in London, see Peck and Norman, 1999). The teamworking book in this series (Jelphs and Dickinson, 2008) provides further discussion about different professional discourses within teams so we say little more about this topic here, with the exception of a final point regarding leadership and professional discourses.

One implication of the existence of these different professional discourses is that they are constituted by professionals who may have a high degree of influence or power within their context (such as clinicians), even though they may not occupy a position of formal authority (and are good examples of Lipsky's street-level bureaucrats). Thus, partnerships need to seek to engage the most appropriate individuals to lead or manage certain procedures at specific times and often these will be individuals who may not always be associated with institutionalised roles.

—

Within this context, the role of dominant professionals, and particularly doctors, is of key importance. In Mintzberg's (1979) words, professional bureaucracies, such as those providing healthcare, 'are not integrated entities. They are collections of individuals who join to draw on the common resources and support services but otherwise want to be left alone' (p 372). Professionals are characterised as having a high degree of autonomy and the ability to resist calls for greater integration. In this context, change is the product of 'successive negotiations [which] take place through a process of partisan mutual adjustment and as a plurality of interest groups operate in decision making areas' (Pettigrew et al, 1992, p 14). In developing this nuanced picture of professional collaboration within healthcare organisations, Denis et al (1999) emphasised three features of collaboration: emergent operating units; differentiated professional influence; and diluted managerial control.

Emergent operating units describe the distinctive forms of coordination among professionals that are associated with different categories of patient–group complexity. Whatever the source of complexity, medical control tends to dominate these operating units. In some cases this takes the form of a hierarchical model, while in others a key coordination mechanism is 'mutual adjustment among professionals' (Denis et al, 1999, p 109). Informal ongoing interactions between professionals are influenced by a range of factors, including tacit rules, mutual trust and 'intrinsic power relationships and incentives', and together produce the stable 'negotiated order' of emergent operating units (Denis et al, 1999, p 110). The operating unit 'is the key part of a professional organization because it is here that critical decisions about the content of work are made by professionals' (p 109). They argue that these semi-autonomous operating units form the de facto elementary structures of healthcare organisations, which are dominated by doctors whose knowledge makes them the de facto team leaders.

This concept has been developed under the 'microsystem' label and has emerged as a focus for clinical quality improvement work (Institute of Medicine, 2001; Nelson et al, 2002). Returning to organisational performance, the traditional autonomy over work practices exercised by senior clinicians has led to wide variations in medical practice, for example, the volume of healthcare provided that cannot be justified in terms of efficacy (Glover, 1938; Wennberg et al, 1987). The actions of these 'unofficial' leaders set a precedent in terms of what is acceptable within particular times and spaces. In order to change internal processes, these professional leaders must be engaged; this will give a clear and symbolic gesture to other members of that profession.

The challenges that follow from the power that resides in such street-level bureaucrats are compounded for leaders by the divergence in professional discourses. Fitzgerald et al (1999) illustrate this well in a study that set out to examine the adoption of clinical change within the acute hospital sector and to identify the 'scientific' and 'non-scientific' factors shaping this adoption. In summary, the most evidence-based change was the least adopted and the least evidence-based change was the most adopted. They identify five key findings from this study and five implications for organisations. These are reproduced in Table 4.3. In essence, however, the research provides compelling support for the suggestion that it is in the processes of organising by leaders that the opportunities for change reside when working with professional groups.

Overall, therefore, given the longevity of and commitment to these disparate professional discourses, it is unlikely that simple exhortation by partnership leaders – even when such exhortations are argued to be evidence-based – is going to be enough to deliver significant shifts in professional practice. Furthermore, the experience of Somerset (Peck et al, 2002b) suggests that simple interventions – such as co-location of professionals – will not be sufficient to deliver the desired outcomes. Rather, more subtle engagement with professional cultures and ways of sense making will need to be combined with innovations in patterns of authority, accountability and procedure in order to achieve the benefits for patients, clients and the public to which partnerships aspire.

Table 4.3: The findings and implications of research by Fitzgerald et al on adoption of evidence-based practice

Finding 1	There was no strong relationship found between the strength of the evidence base and the rate of adoption of the innovation
Implication	Linear models of implementation are seriously misleading and are likely to lead to serious implementation deficits
Finding 2	Scientific evidence is in part a social construction as well as 'objective' data
Implication	There is no such entity as 'the body of evidence' but rather competing bodies of evidence available
Finding 3	There are different forms of evidence differentially accepted by different individuals and occupational groups
Implication	The intergroup issues also need to be addressed explicitly through the construction of linking bodies which bring the different groups involved in the implementation together, preferably within a learning environment and outside the busy daily routine
Finding 4	The data identify specific organisational and social factors that affect the career and outcome of clinical change issues
Implication	The most effective implementation strategies may combine top-down pressure and bottom-up energy
Finding 5	The upper tiers of the NHS, healthcare purchasers, Research and Development and the general management process played only a marginal role in the change process
Implication	There is a need to embed change within the professions themselves

Source: Summarised from Fitzgerald et al (1999)

Reflective exercises

1. Think about a partnership you have experienced or have read about. Which of Meyerson and Martin's perspectives of culture are present within the partnership? What practical implications does this have?

2. Investigate some of the organisational culture measures in Box 4.1 and find which is most appropriate to a partnership (or organisation) you work with on a regular basis. If you can, use this measure. What does this tell you about culture?

3. Think about a partnership you have experience of or have read about. Which different professional cultures are present? What implications do they have for partnership working?

4. Think again about the same partnership. Which ways of organising (outlined in Figure 4.3) are present? What are the ritual forms associated with these forms and what implications does this have for partnership working?

Further reading and resources

Many of the key texts for this chapter are summarised in the relevant section above for readers to explore in more depth as appropriate. However:

- For detailed applications of NDIT to health and social care organisations see Peck and 6's (2006) *Beyond delivery*
- For an introduction to these issues see Schein's (1985) *Organizational culture and leadership*
- For further detail on how to manage this process see Dickinson et al's (2006) review of the merger literature

Useful websites include:

- Aston Organisation Development is a spin-out company from Aston Business School that hosts a wealth of resources including culture resources: www.astonod.com/index.php
- Inter-logics is a multidisciplinary consulting practice specialising in work with complex organisations and multiagency partnerships: www.inter-logics.net/default.aspx

5

Recommendations for policy and practice

It would be to ignore the richness of the preceding discussion to try at this stage to draw out a simple set of lessons – to construct a cookbook after the banquet! However, the challenges, summaries and frameworks we have set out in this text do lead us to make a set of practical recommendations and potential warnings, both for policy and for practice.

For policy makers:

- Although effective leadership and management do have a significant impact on the functioning of interagency collaborations, it is important that leaders' roles are not overstated, and that we are realistic about what types of leadership and management can produce what kinds of results in what sets of circumstances.

- Although it is often suggested that leaders and managers of partnerships need distinct skills and attributes to those operating in more traditional settings, this distinction can be overstated; there are also significant overlaps in the types of tasks and challenges that both sets of leaders and managers will face and these should not be underestimated. This has clear implications for the training and development of these individuals where understanding of the contexts for and nature of partnerships – and thus the sense making and performance that may be most effective – may be as important as the skills and attributes themselves.

- Although formal governance structures are important to some types of settings, we should be wary of the instrumental claims that are made for these processes. Power does not simply reside at the executive level, which means we need to think through in more detail about how it may be exercised to bring about change.

- The importance and implications of the interaction between political, community and organisational leadership should not be underestimated within partnership settings. We need to be clearer about what these roles entail and how these leaders go about coordinating their activities.

For local organisations and frontline services:

- There is a need to be clear about what types of drivers are present in any collaboration. These are important to establish as they influence the form that any collaboration takes and the difficulties that it may encounter.

- Different sorts of partnership require different types of management and leadership, and it is important to consider the aims of the partnership and the types of tasks that they have been set up to address (as both these factors will influence the nature of management and leadership which will be most effective within these settings).

- Regardless of network form, different management and leadership attributes will prove more effective at certain points within the partnership life cycle than others.

- When asked to work in partnership, it is useful for agencies to reflect on the ways in which they and their partners organise themselves and the different values and rituals that are privileged in these organisations. It is important to think through the settlement that will be reached between partners as this has implications for form and the ways in which power may be effectively executed.

Above all, the (often very theoretical) discussions and frameworks in this book suggest that managing and leading in interagency partnerships are difficult, intricate tasks. Rather than falling for the 'easy answers' of the management cookbooks, we hope that this attempt to synthesise and explore the evidence will give a more nuanced, and hopefully more useful, insight.

References

6, P., Goodwin, N., Peck, E. and Freeman, T. (2006) *Managing networks of twenty-first century organisations*, Basingstoke: Palgrave.

6, P., Leat, D., Seltzer, K. and Stoker, G. (2002) *Towards holistic governance: The new reform agenda*, Basingstoke: Palgrave.

Agranoff, R. and McGuire, M. (2001) 'Big questions in public network management research', *Journal of Public Administration Research and Theory*, vol 11, pp 295-326.

Aldrich, H. (1979) *Organizations and environments*, Englewood Cliffs, NJ: Prentice-Hall.

Aldrich, H. and Herker, D. (1977) 'Boundary spanning roles and organization structure', *The Academy of Management Review*, vol 2, pp 217-30.

Alimo-Metcalfe, B. (1998) *Effective leadership*, London: Local Government Board.

Alimo-Metcalfe, B. and Alban-Metcalfe, J. (2003) 'Stamp of greatness', *Health Service Journal*, vol 113, pp 28-32.

Alvesson, M. and Sveningsson, S. (2003) 'The great disappearing act: difficulties in doing "leadership"', *Leadership Quarterly*, vol 14, pp 359-81.

Anderson-Wallace, M. (2005) 'Working with structure', in E. Peck (ed) *Organisational development in healthcare: Approaches, innovations, achievements*, Abingdon: Radcliffe Medical Publishing.

Armistead, C., Pettigrew, P. and Aves, S. (2007) 'Exploring leadership in multi-sectoral partnerships', *Leadership*, vol 3, pp 211-30.

Audit Commission (2005) *Governing partnerships: Bridging the accountability gap*, London: Audit Commission.

Bachrach, P. and Baratz, M.S. (1962) 'The two faces of power', *American Political Science Review*, vol 56, pp 947-52.

Balloch, S. and Taylor, M. (eds) (2001) *Partnership working: Policy and practice*, Bristol: The Policy Press.

Bardach, E. (1998) *Getting agencies to work together: The practice and theory of managerial craftsmanship*, Washington, DC: Brookings Institute.

Barnes, M., Sullivan, H. and Matka, E. (2004) *The development of collaborative capacity in Health Action Zones. A final report from the national evaluation*, Birmingham: University of Birmingham.

Barnes, M., Bauld, L., Benzeval, M., Judge, K., Mackenzie, M. and Sullivan, H. (2005) *Health Action Zones: Partnerships for health equity*, London: Routledge.

Barrett, G., Sellman, D. and Thomas, J. (eds) (2005) *Interprofessional working in health and social care: Professional perspectives*, Basingstoke: Palgrave.

Bass, B. (1960) *Leadership, psychology, and organizational behaviour*, New York: Harper.

Bass, B. (1974 edn) *Bass and Stogdill's handbook of leadership: Theory, research and managerial applications*, New York: Free Press.

Bass, B. (1990 edn) *Bass and Stogdill's handbook of leadership: Theory, research and managerial applications*, New York: Free Press.

Bate, P., Khan, R. and Pye, A. (2000) 'Towards a culturally sensitive approach to organizational structuring: where organization design meets organization development', *Organization Science*, vol 11, pp 197–211.

Bate, S.P. and Robert, G. (2002) 'Knowledge management and communities of practice in the private sector: lessons for modernizing the national health service in England and Wales', *Public Administration*, vol 80, pp 643–63.

BBC (British Broadcasting Corporation) (2003) 'Trusts to take over child care', 28 January (www.bbc.co.uk).

BBC (2005) '"Home alone" deaths for thousands', 29 December (www.bbc.co.uk).

Bell, C. (1997) *Ritual: Dimensions and perspectives*, Oxford: Oxford University Press.

Bellandi, D. (1999) 'Integrating systems for chronic care', *Modern Health Care*, vol 29, p 32.

Bennis, W.G. (1994) *On becoming a leader*, New York: Perseus Press.

Berger, P.L. and Luckmann, T. (1966) *The social construction of reality: A treatise its the sociology of knowledge*, Garden City, NY: Anchor Books.

Bernick, C.L. (2001) 'When your culture needs a makeover', *Harvard Business Review*, vol 79, pp 53-61.

Bevan, H. (2005) 'On the challenges of reform' (www.institute.nhs. uk, 16/10/2005).

Blackler, F. (2006) 'Chief executives and the modernization of the English National Health Service', *Leadership*, vol 2, pp 5-30.

Blake, R. and Moulton, J. (1965) 'A 9,9 approach for increasing organizational productivity', in M. Sherif (ed) *Intergroup relations and leadership*, New York: Wiley.

Boje, D. and Dennehey, R. (1999) *Managing in a post-modern world*, Dubaque, IA: Kendall-Hunt.

Bolden, R. and Gosling, J. (2006) 'Is the NHS Leadership Qualities framework missing the wood for the trees?', in A. Casbeer, A. Harrison and A. Mark (eds) *Innovations in health care: A reality check*, Basingstoke: Palgrave.

Boyne, G.A. (2002) 'Public and private management: what's the difference?', *Journal of Management Studies*, vol 39, pp 97-122.

Briggs Myers, I. (2000) *Introduction to type*, Oxford: Oxford Psychologists Press.

Brown, M.M., O'Toole, L.J. and Brundley, J.L. (1998) 'Implementing information technology in government: an empirical assessment of the role of local partnerships', *Journal of Public Administration Research and Theory*, vol 8, pp 499-525.

Bryman, A. (1992) *Charisma and leadership in organizations*, London: Sage Publications.

Burr, V. (1995) *An introduction to social constructionism*, London: Routledge.

Burstow, P. (2005) *Dying alone: Assessing isolation, loneliness and poverty* (www.paulburstow.org.uk).

Cameron, A. and Lart, R. (2003) 'Factors promoting and obstacles hindering joint working: a systematic review of the research evidence', *Journal of Integrated Care*, vol 11, issue 2, pp 9-17.

Carnevale, D. (2003) *Organizational development in the public sector*, Boulder, CO: Westview Press.

Child, J. and Faulkner, D. (1998) *Strategies of cooperation*, Cambridge, MA: Oxford University Press.

Clegg, S. (1989) *Frameworks of power*, London: Sage Publications.

Clegg, S., Kornberger, M. and Pitsis, T. (2005) *Managing and organizations: An introduction to theory and practice*, London: Sage Publications.

Collins, J. (2001) *Good to great: Why some companies make the leap and others don't*, London: Random House.

Cooper, L., Coote, A., Davies, A. and Jackson, C. (1995) *Voices off? Tackling the democratic deficit in health*, London: Institute for Public Policy Research.

Cornforth, C. (2003) *The governance of public and non-profit organisations – What do boards do?*, London: Routledge.

Coulson, A. (2005) 'A plague on all your partnerships: theory and practice in regeneration', *International Journal of Public Sector Management*, vol 18, pp 151-63.

Craig, D. (2004) *Building on partnership: Sustaining local collaboration and devolved coordination*, LPG Research Paper No 15, Auckland: University of Auckland.

Cresswell, T. (1996) *In place/out of place: Geography, ideology, and transgression*, Minneapolis, MN: University of Minnesota Press.

Dahl, R.A. (1957) 'The concept of power', *Behavioural Science*, vol 2, pp 201-15.

Davidson, D. and Peck, E. (2005) 'Organisational development and the "repertoire" of healthcare leaders', in E. Peck (ed) *Organisational development in healthcare: Approaches, innovations, achievements*, Abingdon: Radcliffe Medical Publishing.

Davies, H.T., Nutley, S. and Mannion, R. (2000) 'Organisational culture and quality of health care', *Quality in Health Care*, vol 9, pp 111-19.

Davies, J. (2004) '"Conjuncture or disjuncture?", An institutionalist analysis of local regeneration partnerships in the UK', *International Journal of Urban and Regional Research*, vol 28, pp 570-85.

Degeling, P. (1995) 'The significance of "sectors" in calls for urban health intersectorialism: an Australian perspective', *Policy & Politics*, vol 23, pp 289-301.

Denis, J.-L., Lamonthe, L., Langley, A. and Valette, A. (1999) 'The struggle to redefine boundaries in health care systems', in D. Drock, M. Powell and C. Hinings (eds) *Restructuring the professional organisation*, London: Routledge.

DH (Department of Health) (1998) *Partnership in action: New opportunities for joint working between health and social services*, London: DH.

Dickinson, H. (2008) *Evaluating outcomes in health and social care*, Bristol: The Policy Press.

Dickinson, H., Peck, E. and Davidson, D. (2007) 'Opportunity seized or missed? A case study of leadership and organizational change in the creation of a care trust', *Journal of Interprofessional Care*, vol 21, pp 503-13.

Dickinson, H., Peck, E. and Smith, J. (2006) *Leadership in organisational transition – What can we learn from the research evidence?*, Birmingham: Health Services Management Centre.

Douglas, M. (1982) *Essays in the sociology of perception*, London: Routledge.

Dowling, B., Powell, M. and Glendinning, C. (2004) 'Conceptualising successful partnerships', *Health and Social Care in the Community*, vol 12, no 4, pp 309-17.

Dubrin, A. (2004) *Leadership: Research findings, practice and skills*, New York: Houghton Mifflin.

Dunleavy, P. (1991) *Democracy, bureaucracy and public choice*, New York: Harvester Wheatsheaf.

Durkheim, E. (1951 [1891]) *Suicide: A study in sociology*, London: Routledge.

Emery, F. and Trist, E. (1973) *Towards a social ecology*, New York: Plenum.

Ettore, B. (2000) 'Alliances multiply, but most fail to deliver', *Management Review*, vol 89, p 7.

Evetts, J. (1999) 'Professionalisation and professionalism: issues for interprofessional care', *Journal of Interprofessional Care*, vol 13, pp 119-28.

Exworthy, M. and Powell, M. (2004) 'Big windows and little windows: implementation in the "congested state"', *Public Administration*, vol 82, pp 263-81.

Ferlie, E., Pettigrew, A., Ashburner, L. and Fitzgerald, L. (1996) *The new public management in action*, Oxford: Oxford University Press.

Feyerabend, P. (2000) *Conquest of abundance: A tale of abstraction versus the richness of being*, Chicago, IL: University of Chicago Press.

Fiedler, F. (1967) *A theory of leadership effectiveness*, New York: McGraw-Hill.

Field, J. and Peck, E. (2003) 'Mergers and acquisitions in the private sector: what are the lessons for health and social services?', *Social Policy and Administration*, vol 37, pp 742-55.

Fitzgerald, L., Ferlie, E., Wood, M. and Hawkins, C. (1999) 'Evidence into practice: an exploratory analysis of the interpretation of evidence', in A. Mark and S. Dopson (eds) *Organisational behaviour in health care: The research agenda*, Basingstoke: Macmillan.

Fleming, L. and Waguespack, D.M. (2007) 'Brokerage, boundary spanning, and leadership in open innovation communities', *Organization Science*, vol 18, pp 165-80.

Freeman, T. and Peck, E. (2007) 'Performing governance: a partnership board dramaturgy', *Public Administration*, vol 85, issue 4, pp 907-29.

Friend, J.K., Power, J.M. and Yewlett, C.J.L. (1974) *Public planning: The inter-corporate dimension*, London: Tavistock.

Fullan, M. (2001) *Leading in a culture of change*, San Francisco, CA: Jossey-Bass.

Fulop, N., Protopsaltis, G., King, A., Allen, P., Hutchings, A. and Normand, C. (2005) 'Changing organisations: a study of the context and processes of mergers of health care providers in England', *Social Science & Medicine*, vol 60, no 1, pp 119-30.

Gemmill, G. and Oakley, J. (1992) 'Leadership: an alienating social myth?', *Human Relations*, vol 45, pp 113-29.

George, J. (2000) 'Emotions and leadership: the role of emotional intelligence', *Human Relations*, vol 53, pp 1027-55.

Giddens, A. (1993) 'Structuration theory: past, present and future', in C. Bryant and D. Jary (eds) *Giddens' theory of structuration*, London: Routledge.

Glasby, J. and Dickinson, H. (2008) *Partnership working in health and social care*, Bristol: The Policy Press.

Glasby, J. and Peck, E. (2003) *Care trusts: Partnership working in action*, Abingdon: Radcliffe Medical Press.

Glasby, J. and Peck, E. (2004) *Integrated working and governance: A discussion paper*, Leeds: Integrated Care Network.

Glasby, J. and Peck, E. (2006) *We have to stop meeting like this: The governance of inter-agency partnerships*, Leeds: Integrated Care Network.

Glasby, J., Smith, J. and Dickinson, H. (2006) *Creating 'NHS Local': A new relationship between PCTs and local government*, Birmingham: Health Services Management Centre.

Glendinning, C., Powell, M. and Rummery, K. (2002b) *Partnerships, New Labour and the governance of welfare*, Bristol: The Policy Press.

Glendinning, C., Hudson, B., Hardy, B. and Young. R. (2002a) *National evaluation of notifications for the use of the Section 31 partnership flexibilities in the Health Act 1999: Final project report*, Leeds/Manchester: Nuffield Institute for Health/National Primary Care Research and Development Centre.

Glover, A.J. (1938) 'The incidence of tonsil-lectomy in school children', *Proceedings of the Royal Society of Medicine*, 27 May, pp 1219-36.

Goffman, E. (1959) *The presentation of self in everyday life*, Garden City, NY: Doubleday.

Goffman, E. (1974) *Frame analysis: An essay on the organization of experience*, London: Harper and Row.

Goldsmith, S. and Eggers, W. (2004) *Governing by network: The new shape of the public sector*, Washington, DC: Brookings Institute Press.

Goleman, D. (1996) *Emotional intelligence: Why it can matter more than IQ*, London: Bloomsbury.

Gould, L., Ebers, R. and Clinchy, R. (1999) 'The systems psychodynamics of a joint ventures: anxiety, social defenses and the management of mutual dependence', *Human Relations*, vol 52, pp 697-722.

Grint, K. (2000) *The arts of leadership*, Oxford: Oxford University Press.

Grint, K. (2005a) 'Problems, problems, problems: the social construction of "leadership"', *Human Relations*, vol 58, pp 1467-94.

Grint, K. (2005b) *Leadership: Limits and possibilities*, Basingstoke: Palgrave Macmillan.

Hall, S. and Nevin, B. (1998) *Competition, partnership and regeneration: Lessons from three rounds of the Single Regeneration Budget Fund*, Birmingham: Centre for Urban and Regional Studies.

Hardacre, J. and Peck, E. (2005) 'What is organisational development?', in E. Peck (ed) *Organisational development in healthcare: Approaches, innovations, achievements*, Abingdon: Radcliffe Medical Publishing.

Hardy, B., Turrell, A. and Wistow, G. (1992) *Innovations in community care management*, Aldershot: Avebury.

Harrigan, K.R. (1995) 'The role of intercompany cooperation in integrated strategy: strategic alliances and partnering arrangements', *Advances in Strategic Management*, vol 11, p 20.

Harrison, A., Hunter, D., Marnoch, G. and Pollitt, C. (1992) *Just managing: Power and culture in the NHS*, Basingstoke: Macmillan.

Healthcare Commission/CSCI (Commission for Social Care Inspection) (2006) *Joint investigation into the provision of service for people with learning disabilities at Cornwall Partnership NHS Trust*, London: Healthcare Commission.

Hemphill, L., McGreal, S., Berry, J. and Watson, S. (2006) 'Leadership, power and multisector urban: regeneration partnerships', *Urban Studies*, vol 43, pp 59-80.

Hersey, P. and Blanchard, K. (1988) *Management of organisational behaviour: Utilizing human resources*, Englewood Cliffs, NJ: Prentice-Hall.

Hoggett, P. (2006) 'Conflict, ambivalence, and the contested purpose of public organizations', *Human Relations*, vol 59, pp 175-94.

Hood, C. (1995) 'Contemporary public management: a new global paradigm', *Public Policy and Administration*, vol 10, pp 104-17.

Hosking, D. (1988) 'Organizing, leadership and skilful process', *Journal of Management Studies*, vol 25, pp 147-66.

House, R. (1971) 'A path-goal theory of leader effectiveness', *Administrative Science Quarterly*, vol 16, pp 321-38.

Hudson, B. (2000) 'Inter-agency collaboration: a sceptical view', in A. Brechin, H. Brown and M. Eby (eds) *Critical practice in health and social care*, Milton Keynes: Open University Press.

Hudson, B. (2004) 'Care trusts: a sceptical view', in J. Glasby and E. Peck (eds) *Care trusts: Partnership working in action*, Abingdon: Radcliffe Medical Press.

Hudson, B., Exworthy, M. and Peckham, S. (1998) *The integration of localised and collaborative purchasing: A review of the literature and framework for analysis*, Leeds: Nuffield Institute for Health.

Huff, A. (1988) 'Politics and argument as a means of coping with ambiguity and change', in L.R. Pondy, R.J. Boland and H. Thomas (eds) *Managing ambiguity and change*, New York: John Wiley.

Hunter, D.L. (1996) 'The changing roles of health personnel in health and health care management', *Social Science and Medicine*, vol 43, pp 799-808.

Hunter, D.L. (1999) 'Accountability and local democracy', *British Journal of Health Care Management*, vol 1, pp 78-81.

Huxham, C. (1996) 'Collaboration and collaborative advantage', in C. Huxham (ed) *Creating collaborative advantage*, London: Sage Publications.

Huxham, C. and MacDonald, D. (1992) 'Introducing collaborative advantage: achieving interorganizational effectiveness through meta-strategy', *Management Decision*, vol 30, pp 50-6.

Institute of Medicine (2001) *Crossing the quality chasm: A new health system for the 21st century*, Washington, DC: National Academy Press.

Jelphs, K. and Dickinson, H. (2008) *Working in teams*, Bristol: The Policy Press.

Judge, W. and Ryman, J. (2001) 'The shared leadership challenge in strategic alliances: lessons from the US healthcare industry', *Academy of Management Executive*, vol 15, pp 71-9.

Jupp, B. (2000) *Working together: Creating a better environment for cross-sector partnerships*, London: Demos.

Kanter, R.M. (1989) *When giants learn to dance*, New York: Simon & Schuster.

Kanter, R.M. (1994) 'Collaborative advantage: the art of alliances', *Harvard Business Review*, vol 72, pp 96-108.

Katz, D. and Kahn, R.L. (1966) *Organizations and the system concept*, New York: Wiley.

Kickert, W., Klijn, E.-H. and Koppenjan, J.F.M. (1997) *Managing complex networks: Strategies for the public sector*, London: Sage Publications.

Kingdon, J. (1995) *Agendas, alternatives and public policies*, Boston, MD: Little, Brown and Co.

Klein, R. and New, B. (1998) *Two cheers? Reflections on the health of NHS democracy*, London: King's Fund.

Koppenjan, J. and Klijn, E.-H. (2004) *Managing uncertainties in networks*, London: Routledge.

Latour, B. (1996) *Aramis, or the love of technology*, Cambridge, MA: Harvard University Press.

Lawler, J. (2000) 'The rise of managerialism in social work', in E. Harlow and J. Lawler (eds) *Management, social work and change*, London: Ashgate.

Lawler, J. (2004) 'Meaning and being: existentialist concepts in leadership', *International Journal of Management Concepts and Philosophy*, vol 1, pp 61-72.

Leutz, W. (1999) 'Five laws for integrating medical and social services: lessons from the United States and the United Kingdom', *The Milbank Quarterly*, vol 77, no 1, pp 77-110.

Likert, R. (1961) 'An emerging theory of organizations, leadership and management', in L. Petrullo and E. Bass (eds) *Leadership and interpersonal behaviour*, New York: Holt, Rinehart & Winston.

Lin, Y.J. and Wan, T.T.H. (2001) 'Effect of organizational and environmental factors on service differentiation strategy of integrated healthcare networks', *Health Services Management Research*, vol 14, pp 18-26.

Ling, T. (2002) 'Delivering joined-up government in the UK: dimensions, issues and problems', *Public Administration*, vol 80, pp 615-42.

Lipsky, M. (1980) *Street-level bureaucracy: Dilemmas of the individual in public services*, New York: Basic Books.

Luke, J.S. (1997) *Catalytic leadership: Strategies for an interconnected world*, San Francisco, CA: Jossey-Bass.

Lukes, S. (1974) *Power: A radical view*, London: Macmillan.

Lynn, L. (2006) *Public management. Old and new*, London: Routledge.

Lynn, L., Heinrich, C. and Hill, C. (2001) *Improving governance: A new logic for empirical research*, Washington, DC: Georgetown University Press.

Lyons Inquiry (2006) *National prosperity, local choice and civic engagement: A new partnership between central and local government for the 21st century*, Norwich: The Stationery Office.

McCallin, A. (2003) 'Interdisciplinary team leadership: a revisionist approach for an old problem', *Journal of Nursing Management*, vol 11, pp 364-70.

McCray, J. and Ward, C. (2003) 'Editorial notes for November: leading interagency collaboration', *Journal of Nursing Management*, vol 11, pp 361-3.

McCulloch, A. and Parker, C. (2004) 'Inquiries, assertive outreach and compliance: is there a relationship?', in N. Stanley and J. Manthorpe (eds) *The age of inquiry: Learning and blaming in health and social care*, London: Routledge.

McGregor, D. (1966) *Leadership and motivation*, Cambridge, MA: MIT Press.

McGuire, M. (2006) 'Collaborative public management: assessing what we know and how we know it', *Public Administration Review*, vol 66, pp 33-43.

McLaughlin, K., Osborne, S. and Ferlie, E. (2002) *The new public management: Current trends and future prospects*, London: Routledge.

McLeod, H. (2005) 'A review of the evidence on organisational development in healthcare', in E. Peck (ed) *Organisational development in healthcare: An introduction*, Abingdon: Radcliffe Medical Press.

Mangham, I. (2004) 'Leadership and integrity', in J. Storey (ed) *Leadership in organisations: Key issues and trends*, Oxford: Routledge.

Marks, M.L. and Mirvis, P.H. (1992) 'Rebuilding after the merger: dealing with "survivor sickness"', *Organizational Dynamics*, pp 18-32.

Martin, J. (1992) *Culture in organizations: Three perspectives*, Oxford: Oxford University Press.

Maslow, A. (1954) *Motivation and personality*, New York: Harper.

Matka, E., Barnes, M. and Sullivan, H. (2002) 'Health Action Zones: "creating alliances to achieve change"', *Policy Studies*, vol 23, pp 97-106.

Mayo, M. (1997) 'Partnerships for regeneration and community development', *Critical Social Policy*, vol 17, pp 3-26.

Meyerson, D. and Martin, J. (1987) 'Cultural change: an integration of three different views', *Journal of Management Studies*, vol 24, pp 623-43.

Milward, H.B. and Provan, K.G. (2000) 'Governing the hollow state', *Journal of Public Administration Research and Theory*, vol 10, pp 359-79.

Mintzberg, H. (1979) *The structuring of organisations: A synthesis of research*, Englewood Cliffs, NJ: Prentice-Hall.

Mintzberg, H. (1983) *Power in and around organisations*, Englewood Cliffs, NJ: Prentice-Hall.

Mintzberg, H. and van der Heyden, L. (1999) 'Organigraphs: drawing how companies really work', *Harvard Business Review*, vol 77, pp 87-94.

Mitchell, S.M. and Shortell, S.M. (2000) 'The governance and management of effective community health partnerships: a typology for research, policy and practice', *The Milbank Quarterly*, vol 78, pp 241-89.

National Sure Start Evaluation (2005) *Early impacts of Sure Start local programmes on children and families: Report of the Cross-sectional Study of 9-and 36-month Old Children and their Families*, London: The Stationery Office.

Nelson, E., Batalden, P.B., Huber, T.P., Mohr, J.J., Godfrey, M.M., Headrick, L.A. and Wasson, J.H. (2002) 'Microsystems in health care: Part 1. Learning from high-performing front-line clinical units', *Journal on Quality Improvement*, vol 28, pp 472-93.

Noble, G. and Jones, R. (2006) 'The role of boundary-spanning managers in the establishment of public–private partnerships', *Public Administration*, vol 84, pp 891-917.

Norman, I.J. and Peck, E. (1999) 'Working together in adult community mental health services: an inter-professional dialogue', *Journal of Mental Health*, vol 8, pp 217-30.

O'Keeffe, M., Hills, A., Doyle, M. et al (2007) *UK study of abused and neglect of older people: Prevalence survey report*, London: National Centre for Social Research.

O'Leary, R., Gerard, C. and Bingham, L.B. (2006) 'Introduction to the symposium on collaborative public management', *Public Administration Review*, vol 66, pp 6-9.

O'Toole, L.J. (1998) 'The implications for democracy in a networked bureaucratic world', *Journal of Public Administration Research and Theory*, vol 7, pp 443-59.

O'Toole, L.J. and Meier, K.J. (2004) 'Desperately seeking Selznick: cooptation and the dark side of public management in networks', *Public Administration Review*, vol 64, pp 681-93.

ODPM (Office of the Deputy Prime Minister) (2005a) *A process evaluation of the negotiation of pilot local area agreements*, London: ODPM.

ODPM (2005b) *National evaluation of local strategic partnerships issues paper: Leadership in local strategic partnerships*, London: ODPM.

ODPM (2005c) *Evaluation of local strategic partnerships: Interim report*, London: ODPM.

ODPM (2007) *Evidence of savings, improved outcomes, and good practice attributed to local area agreements*, London: ODPM.

OECD (Organisation for Economic Co-operation and Development) (1995) *Governance in transition: Public management reforms in OECD countries*, Paris: OECD.

Osborne, D. and Gaebler, T. (1993) *Reinventing government: How the entrepreneurial spirit is transforming the public sector*, London: Penguin Books.

Parker, M. (2000) *Organisational culture and identity*, London: Sage Publications.

Payne, M. (2000) *Teamwork in multiprofessional care*, Basingstoke: Macmillan.

Peck, E. (1995) 'The performance of an NHS trust board: actors' accounts, minutes of meetings and observation', *British Journal of Management*, vol 6, pp 135-56.

Peck, E. (2002) 'Integrating health and social care', *Managing Community Care*, vol 10, no 3, pp 16-19.

Peck, E. (2006) 'Leadership and its development in healthcare', in K. Walshe and J. Smith (eds) *Healthcare management*, Maidenhead: Open University Press.

Peck, E. and 6, P. (2006) *Beyond delivery: Policy implementation as sense-making and settlement*, Basingstoke: Palgrave.

Peck, E. and Crawford, A. (2004) *'Culture' in partnerships – What do we mean by it and what can we do about it?*, Leeds: Integrated Care Network.

Peck, E. and Dickinson, H. (2008: forthcoming) 'Managing integration: partnership working and organisational culture', in J. Glasby and H. Dickinson (eds) *International health and social care: Partnership working in action*, Oxford: Blackwell Publishing.

Peck, E. and Norman, I.J. (1999) 'Working together in adult community mental health services: exploring inter-professional role relations', *Journal of Mental Health*, vol 8, pp 231-42.

Peck, E. and Wigg, S. (2002) 'Policies, priorities, opportunities and barriers to mental health services: five years of the London managers' survey', *Journal of Mental Health*, vol 15, pp 55-66.

Peck, E., Dickinson, H. and Smith, J. (2006) 'Transforming or transacting? The role of leaders in organisational transition', *British Journal of Leadership in Public Services*, vol 2, pp 4-14.

Peck, E., Gulliver, P. and Towell, D. (2002a) 'Governance of partnership between health and social services: the experience in Somerset', *Health and Social Care in the Community*, vol 10, pp 331-8.

Peck, E., Gulliver, P. and Towell, D. (2002b) *Modernising partnerships: An evaluation of Somerset's innovations in the commissioning and organisation of Mental Health Services*, London: Institute of Applied Health and Social Policy, King's College.

Peck, E., Towell, D. and Gulliver, P. (2001) 'The meanings of "culture" in health and social care: a case study of the combined trust in Somerset', *Journal of Interprofessional Care*, vol 15, pp 319-27.

Peck, E., 6, P., Glasby, J. and Skelcher, C. (2004a) 'Governance and partnerships', *Journal of Integrated Care*, vol 12, pp 3-8.

Peck, E., 6, P., Gulliver, P. and Towell, D. (2004b) 'Why do we keep meeting like this? The board as ritual in health and social care', *Health Services Management Research*, vol 17, pp 100-9.

Peters, T.J. and Waterman, R.H. (1982) *In search of excellence: Lessons from America's best-run companies*, New York: Harper & Row.

Pettigrew, A. (1992) 'On studying managerial élites', *Strategic Management Journal*, vol 13, pp 163-82.

Pettigrew, A., Ferlie, E.B. and McKee, L. (1992) *Shaping strategic change. Making change in large organisations: The case of the National Health Service*, London: Sage Publications.

Pfeffer, J. (1992) *Managing with power*, Boston, MD: Harvard Business School Press.

Pierre, J. and Peters, B.G. (2000) *Governance, politics and the state*, New York: St Martin's Press.

PIU (Performance and Innovation Unit) (2001) *Strengthening leadership in the public sector*, London: Cabinet Office Strategy Unit.

Pollitt, C. (1993) *Managerialism and the public services: The Anglo-American experience*, Oxford: Blackwell.

Pollitt, C. (2000) 'Is the emperor in his underwear? An analysis of the impacts of public management reform', *Public Management*, vol 2, pp 181-99.

Powell, M. and Moon, G. (2001) 'Health Action Zones: the "third way" of a new area-based policy', *Health and Social Care in the Community*, vol 9, pp 43-50.

Poxton, R. (1999) *Working across the boundaries*, London: King's Fund.

Provan, K.G. and Milward, H.B. (1995) 'A preliminary theory of interorganizational network effectiveness: a comparative study of four community mental health systems', *Administrative Science Quarterly*, vol 40, pp 1-33.

Pye, A. (1995) 'Strategy through dialogue and doing: a game of Mornington Crescent?', *Management Learning*, vol 25, pp 445-62.

Pye, A. (2005) 'Leadership and organizing: sensemaking in action', *Leadership*, vol 1, pp 31-50.

Robertson, P.J. (1995) 'Involvement in boundary-spanning activity: mitigating the relationship between work setting and behaviour', *Journal of Public Administration Research and Theory*, vol 5, pp 73-98.

Robinson, F. and Shaw, K. (2000) *Who runs the North-East now? A review and assessment of governance in North East England*, Durham: Department of Sociology and Social Policy, University of Durham.

Rodman, M. (1992) 'Empowering place: multilocality and multivocality', *American Anthropologist*, vol 94, pp 640-56.

Rodríguez, C., Langley, A., Beland, F. and Denis, J.-L. (2007) 'Governance, power, and mandated collaboration in an interorganizational network', *Administration & Society*, vol 39, no 2, pp 150-93.

Rugkåsa, J., Shortt, N. and Boydell, L. (2007) 'The right tool for the task: "boundary spanners" in a partnership approach to tackle fuel poverty in rural Northern Ireland', *Health and Social Care in the Community*, vol 15, pp 221-30.

Rummery, K. and Glendinning, C. (2000) *Primary care and social services: Developing new partnerships for older people*, Abingdon: Radcliffe Medical Press.

Salovey, P. and Mayer, J. (1990) 'Emotional intelligence', *Imagination, Cognition and Personality*, vol 9, pp 185-211.

Schechner, R. (2003) *Performance studies: An introduction*, London: Routledge.

Schein, E. (1985) *Organizational culture and leadership*, San Francisco, CA: Jossey-Bass.

Schwartzman, H. (1989) *The meeting: Gatherings in organisations and communities*, New York: Plenum.

Scott, T., Mannion, R., Davies, H.T. and Marshall, M. (2003a) *Healthcare performance and organisational culture*, Abingdon: Radcliffe Medical Press.

Scott, T., Mannion, R., Davies, H.T. and Marshall, M. (2003b) 'The quantitative measurement of organisational culture in health care: a review of the available instruments', *Health Services Research*, vol 38, pp 923-45.

Scottish Executive (2005) *Delivery through leadership*, Edinburgh: Scottish Executive.

Sermeus, W., Vanheacht, K. and Vleugels, A. (2001) 'The Belgian–Dutch clinical pathway network', *Journal of Integrated Care Pathways*, vol 5, pp 10-14.

Shirley, J. (2000) 'Clinical governance in an independent hospital', *Clinician in Management*, vol 9, pp 229-33.

Sidle, C.C. and Warzynski, C.C. (2003) 'A new mission for business schools: the development of actor-network leaders', *Journal of Education for Business*, pp 40-5.

Simon, H. (1997 [1945]) *Administrative behaviour: A study of decision-making processes in administrative organisations*, New York: Free Press.

Skelcher, C. (2000) 'Changing images of the state: overloaded, hollowed out, congested', *Public Policy and Administration*, vol 15, pp 3-19.

Skelcher, C., Mathur, N. and Smith, M. (2004) *Effective partnership and good governance: Lessons for policy and practice*, Birmingham: Institute of Local Government Studies, University of Birmingham.

Stacey, R. (1999) *Strategic management and organisational dynamics: The challenge of complexity*, London: *Financial Times*.

Steadman, H.J. (1992) 'Boundary spanners: a key component for the effective interactions of the justice and mental health systems', *Law and Human Behaviour*, vol 16, pp 75-87.

Stern, R. and Green, J. (2005) 'Boundary workers and the management of frustration: a case study of two Healthy City partnerships', *Health Promotion International*, vol 20, pp 269–76.

Storey, J. (2004a) *Leadership in organizations: Current issues and key trends*, London: Routledge.

Storey, J. (2004b) 'Signs of change: "damned rascals and beyond"', in J. Storey (ed) *Leadership in organisations: Key issues and trends*, Oxford: Routledge.

Storey, J. (2004c) 'Changing theories of leadership and leadership development', in J. Storey (ed) *Leadership in organisations: Key issues and trends*, Oxford: Routledge.

Sullivan, H. and Skelcher, C. (2002) *Working across boundaries: Collaboration in public services*, Basingstoke: Palgrave.

Sullivan, H., Judge, K. and Sewel, K. (2004) '"In the eye of the beholder": perceptions of local impact in English Health Action Zones', *Social Science and Medicine*, vol 59, pp 1603–12.

Sweeney, K. (2005) 'Emergence, complexity and organisational development', in E. Peck (ed) *Organisational development in healthcare: Approaches, innovations, achievements*, Abingdon: Radcliffe Medical Publishing.

Takeishi, A. (2001) 'Bridging inter- and intra-firm boundaries: management of supplier involvement in automobile product development', *Strategic Management Journal*, vol 22, pp 403–33.

Thompson, G. (1991) 'Comparison between models', in G. Thompson, J. Mitchell, R. Levacic and J. Francis (eds) *Markets, hierarchies and networks: The coordination of social life*, London: Sage Publications.

Thompson, J.D. (1967) *Organizations in action: Social science bases of administrative theory*, New York: McGraw-Hill.

University of East Anglia (2007) *Children's trust pathfinders: Innovative partnerships for improving the well-being of children and young people*, Norwich: University of East Anglia in Association with the National Children's Bureau.

Vangen, S. and Huxham, C. (2003) 'Enacting leadership for collaborative advantage: dilemmas of ideology and pragmatism in the activities of partnership managers', *British Journal of Management*, vol 14, pp 61-76.

Volkoff, O., Chan, Y.E. and Newson, P.E.F. (1999) 'Leading the development and implementation of collaborative interorganizational systems', *Information and Management*, vol 35, pp 63-75.

Vroom, V. and Jago, A. (1988) *The new leadership: Managing participation in organisations*, Englewood Cliffs, NJ: Prentice-Hall.

Vroom, V. and Yetton, P. (1973) *Leadership and decision-making*, Pittsburgh, PA: University of Pittsburgh Press.

Wade, E., Smith, J., Peck, E. and Freeman, T. (2006) *Commissioning in the reformed NHS: Policy into practice*, Birmingham: Health Services Management Centre.

Wan, T.T.H., Ma, A. and Lin, Y.J. (2001) 'Integration and the performance of health care networks: do integration strategies enhance efficiency, profitability, and image?', *International Journal of Integrated Care*, vol 1 (www.ijic.org).

Warner, M., Gould, N. and Jones, A. (2003) 'Community Health Alliances through Integrated Networks (CHAIN). Reporting project progress in South Wales with reference to the National Service Framework for older people', Paper presented to the IJIC/WHO 3rd International Conference on Integrated Care, Barcelona, February.

Weick, K. (1995) *Sensemaking in organizations*, London: Sage Publications.

Weiss, E.S., Anderson, R.M. and Lasker, R.D. (2002) 'Making the most of collaboration: exploring the relationship between partnership synergy and partnership functioning', *Health Education and Behaviour*, vol 29, pp 683-98.

Wennberg, J.E., Roos, N. and Sola, L. (1987) 'Use of claims data systems to evaluate health care outcomes: mortality and reoperation following prostatectomy', *Journal of the American Medical Association*, vol 257, pp 933-6.

Wheatley, M. (2001) *Leadership and the new science*, San Francisco, CA: Berrett-Koehler.

Wildridge, V., Childs, S., Cawthra, L. and Madge, B. (2004) 'How to create successful partnerships – a review of the literature', *Health Information and Libraries and Journal*, vol 21, pp 3-19.

Williams, P. (2002) 'The competent boundary spanner', *Public Administration*, vol 80, pp 103-24.

Willumsen, E. (2006) 'Leadership in interprofessional collaboration – the case of childcare in Norway', *Journal of Interprofessional Care*, vol 20, pp 403-13.

Winkler, J. (1974) 'The two faces of capitalism', *The Director*, vol 26, pp 91-4.

Winkler, J. (1975) 'Company directors ... or corporate knights', *The Director*, vol 27, pp 85-7.

Wistow, G. and Hardy, B. (1991) 'Joint management in community care', *Journal of Management in Medicine*, vol 5, pp 40-8.

Wistow, G. and Waddington, E. (2006) 'Learning from doing: implications of the Barking and Dagenham experiences for integrating health and social care', *Journal of Integrated Care*, vol 14, pp 8-18.

Zaleznik, A. (1992) 'Managers and leaders: are they different?', *Harvard Business Review*, vol 3, pp 126-38.

Zimmerman, B.J., Lindberg, C. and Plsek, P.E. (1998) *Edgeware: Insights from complexity science for health care leaders*, Dallas, TX: VHA Publishing.

Index

NOTE: Page numbers followed by *fig* and *tab* indicate information is to be found in a figure or a table.

A

accountability
and new public management 14
and role ambiguity 53-4
Action Zones 42
see also Health Action Zones
actor network theory 73
advocacy leadership approaches 46, 47, 55-6, 66, 79
Agranoff, R. 53
agreement/uncertainty matrix 81-2
Alimo-Metcalfe, B. 74-5
Alvesson, M. 23
ambiguity model of culture 84-5, 86
Anderson-Wallace, M. 1
Armistead, C. 16-17, 50-1, 54-5, 62
asymmetrical perceptions of legitimacy 32*tab*, 64, 71, 89-91
asymmetrical power relations 32*tab*, 71, 91-8
audience and leadership 69-71
autonomy of medical professionals 100-1

B

Bachrach, P. 92
Baratz, M.S. 92
Bardach, E. 46, 47, 66
Barnes, M. 42, 52
Bass, B. 37
Bate, P. 86
Bate, S.P. 45
behavioural leadership 24*tab*

Belgian-Dutch Clinical Pathway Network 44
'big windows and little windows' approach 82-3
Blanchard, K. 26
boards and governance 61-4
symbolic role 64-6, 70
'boundary spanners' 1, 3, 6-8, 24, 35
and network forms 37-48
and role ambiguity 53-4
Boyne, G.A. 12, 52
brokers *see* social brokers; 'strategic brokers'
Brown, M.M. 45
Bryman, A. 27
bureaucracy
and medical profession 100, 101
and NHS networks 44-5

C

care trusts 80, 90
'champions' as leaders 6, 50
charismatic leadership model 26-7, 35, 48, 50
'classical' and network management 36*tab*
Clegg, S. 91, 92-3
Climbié, Victoria xi
collaboration
barriers to 4-6
evidence and failure of 3-6
and hierarchical management 1, 10-11, 42, 80
see also partnership working
collaborative advantage 39-40
collaborative public management 21

'collaborative thuggery' 35, 47-8
collective learning 44
Collins, Jim 35
commissioning 10, 72
    split from providing 11-12,
        15-16
commitment as leadership attribute
    32tab, 52, 53, 55, 56, 71
communities of practice 45
community: leadership from within
    43, 74, 106
competitiveness and network form
    38, 39
complex problems and partnerships
    2
    see also 'wicked problems'
complexity theory 81-2
contingency theory and leadership
    26
Cornforth, C. 62, 63tab, 65
corporate governance 60-1
Cresswell, T. 73
critical problems 21, 22
culture
    challenge of incompatible
        culture 32tab, 84-9
    cultural management/change
        86-9
    divergent professional discourses
        99-102
customer focus as leadership
    attribute 32tab, 42, 53, 55

D
Dahl, R.A. 92
Davidson, D. 14
Davies, H.T. 88
Davies, J. 44
'democratic deficit' in NHS 72,
    89-91
Denis, J.-L. 100

depth/breadth partnership matrix
    9-10, 16
Dickinson, Helen 2-3, 3-4, 9-11,
    84, 99
difference model of culture 84, 85,
    86
'distributed leadership' 28
divergent professional discourses
    32tab, 99-102
doctors and professional discourse
    100
Douglas, Mary 92
drivers for partnerships 17-18, 106
    and research evidence 31, 32tab,
        33, 55
Durkheim, Émile 92-3

E
'earned autonomy' 26
ecological networks 18tab, 37,
    39-40
Eggers, W. 49
emergent operating units 100
Emery, F. 80
'emotional intelligence' 25
enclave form of social organisation
    19fig, 94-5fig, 96, 98, 99
enclave networks 19fig, 20, 52
entrepreneur as leadership attribute
    32tab, 38, 50, 53
'entrepreneurs of power' 6
entrepreneurship and boundary
    spanners 7
evidence-based practice
    and professional discourses 101,
        102tab
    see also research
exploitation of niche networks
    18tab, 39-40
Exworthy, M. 82, 83

F

facilitative leadership approaches
46-7, 48, 66
   attributes of leaders 48-56
Ferlie, E. 61
financial barriers to collaboration
5, 80
financial networks 18*tab*
Fitzgerald, L. 101, 102*tab*
Fleming, L. 45-6
framing problems 67, 81, 82, 83
Freeman, T. 62, 70-1
Fullan, M. 27, 28

G

Gaebler, T. 12-13, 14
Gemmill, G. 34
George, J. 25
Glasby, Jon 2-3, 3-4, 9-11, 72
Goffman, E. 70
Goldsmith, S. 49
Gould, L. 54
governance 59-66, 105-6
   good governance 64-6
   research evidence 61-4
   symbolic role 64-6, 70
'great man' leadership model 24-5
Green, A. 2
Grint, K. 26, 27, 28, 47, 80-1

H

hard power 22
Hardy, B. 4-5, 89
Health Action Zones 33, 34, 41,
42, 52
Hemphill, L. 44
Hersey, P. 26
hierarchical management approach
1-2, 10-11
   bureaucracy and networks in
   NHS 44-5
   middle managers as barrier 42

new public management
   critique 12
   and partnerships 16, 80
hierarchical networks 19*fig*, 20
hierarchy form of social
   organisation 19*fig*, 93, 94-5*fig*,
   98
Hudson, B. 80
Huxham, C. 35, 39, 40, 46-8, 51, 53

I

incompatible culture and values
32*tab*, 84-9
individualism form of social
   organisation 19*fig*, 93, 94-5*fig*
individualistic networks 19*fig*, 20,
39
individuals
   and effective partnerships 42
   and leadership approaches 25-6,
   34, 35-6, 48
information-sharing networks 44-5
innovation and boundary spanners
7
institutional networks 18*tab*, 33
integration model of culture 84,
85, 86
integrity as leadership attribute
32*tab*, 51, 56, 71
interpersonal skills 7, 8, 48-9
isolate form of social organisation
19*fig*, 94-5*fig*, 96, 98
isolate networks 19*fig*, 20

J

JCB, Somerset 62, 64, 98
Jelphs, K. 99
joint consultative committees
(JCCs) 89
joint planning arrangements 89
Jones, R. 6

K

Kahn, R.L. 38
Kanter, R.M. 4, 39-40, 51
Katz, D. 38
Kickert, W. 36
Kingdon, J. 82-3
Klijn, E.-H. 49
Koppenjan, J. 49

L

lack of shared framework 32*tab*, 79-83
Latour, B. 74
Lawler, J. 14, 34
leadership *see* management and leadership
learning networks 38-9, 43-5, 52
legitimacy
    as barrier to collaboration 5
        asymmetrical perceptions of 32*tab*, 64, 71, 89-91
    and governance 60, 64, 65
    voluntary nature of partnerships 51
life cycle of partnerships 51, 53, 55, 106
Lipsky, M. 28, 99
local authorities
    and asymmetrical perceptions of legitimacy 89-91
    and place making 72-3
local level partnerships 52, 79-102, 106
local strategic partnerships (LSPs) 43, 64, 74
Luke, J.S. 50
Lukes, S. 91, 92
Lynn, L. 13, 60
Lyons Inquiry 72-3

M

McCray, J. 6, 79

McGuire, M. 11, 53
McLeod, H. 45
macro-economic networks 18*tab*
maintenance of partnerships 44
management and leadership
    frameworks and concepts 79-102
    hot topics and emerging issues 59-76
    lack of definition of leadership 23
    leadership as 'answer to everything' 33-5
    leadership/management distinction 21-2
    and new public management 14
    of partnerships 54-5
        attributes of leaders 31, 32*tab*, 33, 48-56, 105
        boundary spanners' role 6-8
        challenges 31, 32*tab*, 33, 64, 79-102
        compared with single organisations 53-5, 56
        evidence base 2-3, 35-7
        and failure of collaboration 4-6
        governance 62, 64, 105-6
        and leadership attributes 48-56, 105
        leadership and stages of partnership 43, 53
        recommendations 105-6
        research evidence 2-3, 4-6, 35-7
    research 31-56
    theory of 1, 21-9, 66-71
        and power 91-7
    see also boundary spanners; new public management
'manipulative' leadership 48, 66

markets 11, 16
Marks, M.L. 84
Martin, J. 84-5
Mayo, M. 50
medical profession autonomy 100-1
Meier, K.J. 35
mergers and acquisitions 4, 88
Meyerson, D. 84-5
'microsystems' 100
'middle managers' as barrier 42
Milward, H.B. 38-9
Mintzberg, Henry 82, 92, 100
Mirvis, P.H. 84
Mitchell, S.M. 33
Myers Brigg Type Inventory 25

N

'negotiated order' 80, 100
neo-Durkheimian institutional
    theory (NDIT) 19-20, 92-7
networker as leadership attribute
    32tab, 48-50, 53, 55
networks and partnerships 3, 16-21
    'classical' and network
        management 36tab
    health and social care markets
        11
    negative impacts 35, 40
    and new public management
        11-12
    and organisational form 19-20
    and place making 73
    types of networks 17, 18tab,
        37-48, 55
New Labour
    and leadership 23, 24-5
new public management (NPM)
    3, 11-16
NHS
    boards and governance 61,
        89-91
    bureaucracy and networks 44-5

culture and social care partners
    85, 88
'democratic deficit' 72, 89-91
unconditional acceptance of
    importance of leadership 34
niches see exploitation of niche
    networks
Noble, G. 6

O

Oakley, J. 34
ODPM (Office of the Deputy
    Prime Minister) 43, 64, 74
OECD (Organisation for
    Economic Co-operation and
    Development) 12
O'Leary, R. 21
optimism and partnership working
    2, 47
Organisation for Economic
    Co-operation and Development
    (OECD) 12
organisational culture 84
Osborne, D. 12-13, 14
O'Toole, L.J. 35
outcomes: evaluation of
    collaboration 3-6

P

Parker, M. 86
partnership boards 62, 64, 89-91
partnership life cycle 51, 53, 56, 106
partnership working xi-xv
    definition of partnerships 16-17
    forms of partnerships 9-11
        network forms 37-48
    and networks 16-21
    stages of 43
        see also partnership life cycle
        see also management and
            leadership: of partnerships

path-dependency leadership
approaches 56
path-goal theory and leadership 26
PCTs (primary care trusts) 72
Peck, E. 14, 52, 61, 88
culture and partnerships 84, 85
depth/breadth matrix 9
leadership models 23-4
performance of leadership 70-1
Somerset JCB 62, 98
Somerset Mental Health
Partnership 39, 41-2, 44, 85,
101
performance and leadership 48, 66,
69-71
personal exchanges *see*
interpersonal skills
personal networks 18*tab*, 34
personal-situational leadership
approach 24*tab*, 25
personality of boundary spanners 8
Peters, B.G. 12
Pettigrew, A. 61-2, 65, 100
Pfeffer, J. 91
Pierre, J. 12
'place making' and leadership 16,
72-6
policy
and 'big windows' approach
82-3
and governance 60, 105-6
and partnership working xiv-xv,
16
recommendations 105-6
political leadership 43, 74-5, 106
Pollitt, C. 34
'post-transformational' leadership 7,
24*tab*, 27-8
Powell, M. 82, 83
power 105-6

asymmetrical power relations
32*tab*, 71, 91-8
and management/leadership
distinction 21, 22
Poxton, R. 52
practice-based commissioning 16
predictability as leadership attribute
32*tab*, 38, 51-2, 53, 56
private sector
boards and governance 61-2
collaboration failures 4
and commitment of leaders 52
problem solving/problem sharing
networks 18*tab*, 34, 38-9, 41-3,
45
problems
and management/leadership
distinction 21-2
and networks 18*tab*, 34, 38-9,
41-3, 45
see also 'wicked problems'
procedural barriers to collaboration
5
professional barriers to
collaboration 5
divergent discourses as challenge
32*tab*, 99-102
Project CHAIN 44
'project champions' 6
Provan, K.G. 38-9
psychological profiling leadership
approach 24*tab*, 25
public sector/public services
and commitment of leaders 52
and governance 59-66
and hierarchical management
approach 10-11
and new public management
11-13, 15-16
see also commissioning services
Pye, A. 23

R

regeneration partnerships 90

relational competence as leadership attribute 32*tab*, 34, 48, 51, 55, 69 *see also* interpersonal skills

'requisite variety' 33

resource exchange networks 18*tab*, 37-9, 80

restored behaviour 69

'reticulists' 6, 7

ritual form and social organisation 95*fig*, 98

ritual performance 69, 70, 71

Robert, G. 45

Rodríguez, C. 11

role ambiguity 53-4

S

Schechner, R. 69, 71

Scott, T. 86-7, 88-9

Scottish Executive 23

senior managers 1, 6

'sense making' and leadership 27-8, 67-8, 71
and place making 73-4, 76
and social organisation 93, 96

Sermeus, W. 44

shared framework 32*tab*, 79-83

shared leadership 35-6

Shortell, S.M. 33

Sidle, C.C. 73

situational leadership approach 24*tab*, 25

6, Perri 17, 18*tab*, 19, 37-8, 39, 41, 43-4, 54, 98

Skelcher, C. 15, 50, 51, 52, 60
boundary spanners 7, 8
governance 62, 65, 90

social brokerage 46, 93

social constructionism 66-8, 74, 80

social integration 93-6

social organisation theory 19-20, 92-8

social regulation 93-6

socialisation of professions 99

soft power 22

Somerset JCB 62, 64, 98

Somerset Mental Health Partnership 38-9, 41-2, 44, 85, 101

Stacey, Ralph 81-2

stakeholders and place making 73, 74, 76

status as barrier to collaboration 5

Steadman, H.J. 6

Stern, R. 2

Storey, J. 27, 75

'strategic brokers' 6

structural barriers to collaboration 5

structural change and culture 86

Sullivan, H. 2, 7, 8, 50, 51, 52, 60, 90

Sveningsson, S. 23

Sweeney, K. 82

synergy and leadership 33

T

Takeishi, A. 39

tame problems 21, 22

technological determinist networks 18*tab*

technology contingency networks 18*tab*

technology-driven networks 18*tab*, 45-8

theories of management and leadership 1, 21-9, 66-71, 91-7

Thompson, J.D. 37, 38, 39

trait theory 24-5

transaction costs 38

'transformational' leadership model 7, 13, 24
aspirational dimension 47

charismatic leadership 26-7, 35
and networking skills 48
political dimension 74-5
and research evidence 34
Trist, E. 80
trust
and boundary spanners 8, 46
lack of trust and social
brokerage 46
and leadership attributes 50-1,
56

V

values: challenge of incompatible
culture and values 32*tab*, 84-9
Vangen, S. 35, 46-8, 51, 53
vertical integration 40
Volkoff, O. 45
voluntary nature of partnerships
51, 52
Vroom, V. 26

W

Waddington, E. 85
Wade, E. 72
Waguespack, D.M. 45-6
Ward, C. 6, 79
Warner, M. 44
Warzynski, C.C. 73
Weick, K. 27-8, 67-8, 69
Weiss, E.S. 33
Wheatley, Margaret 82
'wicked problems'
framing 67, 81, 82, 83
and governance 60
and management/leadership
distinction 21-2
and partnership working 2, 15,
41-3, 81-3
Wigg, S. 52
Williams, P. 7-8, 48-9
Willumsen, E. 49

Winkler, J. 61
Wistow, G. 85, 89

Z

Zimmerman, B.J. 82